# EINKORN

# EINKORN

## RECIPES FOR NATURE'S ORIGINAL WHEAT

### CARLA BARTOLUCCI

Photographs by Clay McLachlan

Clarkson Potter/Publishers
New York

Published in the United States by
Clarkson Potter/Publishers, an imprint
of the Crown Publishing Group, a
division of Penguin Random House,
LLC, New York.

www.crownpublishing.com
www.clarksonpotter.com

Library of Congress Cataloging-in-
Publication Data

Bartolucci, Carla.

  Einkorn / Carla Bartolucci ;
photographs by Clay McLachlan. —
First edition.

    pages cm

  Includes index.

1. Cooking (Wheat) 2. Wheat—
Heirloom varieties. I. Title.

  TX809.W45B37 2015

  641.6′311—dc23

  2014040192

ISBN 978-0-8041-8647-6
eBook ISBN 978-0-8041-8648-3

Printed in China

Book design by La Tricia Watford
Cover design by Jess Morphew
Cover photographs by Clay McLachlan

14

First Edition

TO MY GIRLS, GIULIA AND LIVIA—
ALWAYS REMEMBER THAT
ON THE OTHER SIDE OF
EACH CHALLENGE IN LIFE
THERE LIES SOMETHING BEAUTIFUL
AND UNEXPECTED

# CONTENTS

# PREFACE

**MY PARENTS WERE AMAZING TALENTS IN THE KITCHEN,** and both children of Italian-born immigrants. My mother loved people by feeding them, and she never seemed to make a mistake in our little Connecticut kitchen. She understood how flavors came together—every dish she served made my childhood a little more special.

My father only cooked on Saturdays, but he was no less skilled than my mother. He would greet his guests with freshly harvested clams and oysters on a bed of ice, accompanied by homemade cocktail sauce, and he dressed his tuna and fennel salad with lemon juice and olive oil. Though a bricklayer, he dreamed of being a fisherman and kept a lobster boat as a hobby. My parents also loved to forage for wild dandelions, which was definitely out of the ordinary in our small coastal town. They made a memorable frittata as well as a fresh dandelion salad, and they prepared skillets of fresh artichokes just as my father's mother had done in her small fishing village in the Marche region.

Mom and Dad taught us how to love bitter greens and other child-unfriendly vegetables, and their food tasted so fabulous that we never complained or refused. Our steamy little kitchen was the center of our life. For my seventh birthday, I invited my entire class over for my first real party. I know now that my parents worked hard that day, but everything seemed effortless as they brought out trays of pizza to my rowdy little friends. Those kids had never tasted anything like that pizza before and went crazy for it. For the first time, I realized that I could be proud of my Italian heritage.

My own introduction to Italy came at age sixteen. I fell in love with the country at my first meal—a breakfast on the terrace of crusty bread, homemade marmalade from heirloom apricots, eggs with deep orange yolks, and fresh figs from a huge tree that grew over the balcony. I returned to Italy in 1987 for my junior year abroad at the University of Bologna, where I first met my husband, who was born in nearby Modena. Driving through the countryside on a trip to meet his relatives, he pulled over and plucked a beautifully ripened peach from a roadside orchard for me. It seemed like every inch of Italy was made for farming, and I was captivated by the food unfolding beneath my eyes each season.

We later married and settled in Connecticut, where Rodolfo and I turned our combined love of food, farming, and Italy into a profession. In 1996, we began distributing a brand of Italian-made organic foods, bionaturæ, in the United States. As our business grew, we felt the need to be closer to where our products were grown and produced, so we returned to Italy to nurture our business. It was a food lover's homecoming, and we were thrilled to discover that our neighbors were not just buying organic foods but also growing them right on their small farms. A neighbor stored his freshly harvested heirloom wheat with bay leaves to deter pests. A short drive to the mountains could get us a whole prosciutto and leaf lard from heritage pigs that foraged on acorns and lived outdoors. We watched our own olives being pressed into fresh extra-virgin oil in the hills above Lago di Garda. The sight of my neighbor's sheep roaming free on a breathtaking hill made our enjoyment of his fresh ricotta very special.

Yet even as we sought out the best ingredients for our kitchen and the quality of our cooking reached a high point, our oldest daughter's health was at a low point. Starting at age two, Giulia had developed intolerances to dairy and eggs. Even after we eliminated those foods from her diet, something continued to cause problems and her symptoms grew more serious. By age seven, she had a constant dry cough and asthma, frequent tonsillitis, and enlarged lymph nodes, and her hair began falling out. It was then that our family's mission to bring einkorn back began.

Years prior to having children, my husband and I had switched to eating mostly ancient types of wheat like spelt. We never suspected wheat as the culprit, but eventually a doctor in Italy

I view my life in Italy as a gift that has taught me so much about food and farming.

told us that Giulia's symptoms could be caused by what we now know as gluten sensitivity, a disorder experienced by 18 million Americans, and causes symptoms similar to those of celiac disease.

With this new diagnosis, I realized that we would have to change to a completely gluten-free diet. I had just spent a year carefully developing my own sourdough starter to bake bread at home because I had read that souring flour made gluten more digestible. The bread I was baking was the best my family had ever tasted, and I doubted gluten-free bread could ever be that good. While it was a huge relief to know a healthier chapter in Giulia's life was about to begin, there was also sadness about all of the foods she would no longer be able to eat.

Because of our work, my husband and I knew how significantly agriculture had changed over the past century. The era following World War II had changed everything about our food, with the introduction of chemical pesticides and the race to breed new varieties of plants that could grow on a large scale to feed the growing population. We began researching the taxonomy of wheat because we wanted to understand why so many people, including Giulia, were now becoming intolerant to the grain. When we first read about einkorn, the most ancient species of wheat, we got excited and met with the Italian researchers who had been studying it for more than a decade. Einkorn has pure and simple genetics, with fewer chromosomes than other wheat. Einkorn remains more nutritious than modern wheat, containing roughly 30 percent more protein and more antioxidants, B vitamins, and essential dietary and trace minerals. In genetic testing, einkorn was found to lack certain gluten proteins that people with wheat intolerances cannot digest.

Why had we never heard of this ancient grain? In part because there were only a few hundred acres of einkorn being grown worldwide and the grain was on the threshold of extinction— which, not surprisingly, made the relic grain

After eliminating all wheat but einkorn from Giulia's diet, I was surprised to see her symptoms vanish in less than two months.

hard to find. Einkorn's yields are very low, and it is not the easiest wheat to grow or mill; it has a husk that must be removed before milling, which reduces the already low harvest by 40 percent, meaning the yield is just one fifth that of today's wheat. Yet the way einkorn grows is the way wheat is supposed to grow, and as parents, we felt strongly that this was the type of wheat our daughter was meant to eat.

Our family embarked on its own private clinical study, with Giulia as our one and only test subject. When we had einkorn flour, I made everything with it from scratch at home—pasta, bread, crackers, and cookies—and Giulia felt quite good. When she ate other kinds of wheat, her symptoms returned within hours. We witnessed this over and over again and we were astonished by how clear-cut the distinction was. Her asthma, drowsiness, and snoring cleared up in just two months, and I soon realized that it was not bad table manners that had caused her to chew loudly at meals—it was the fact that she couldn't breathe through her nose and had had to eat with her mouth open. The hair she had lost grew back shiny, thick, and curly, and her swollen abdomen flattened. As she healed, slowly her sensitivity to eggs and dairy also subsided. It was not only Giulia who felt better—my husband and I noticed that certain nagging health issues, like an occasional skin rash, tingling in our legs after sitting too long, congestion, and headaches, vanished as well after we switched to einkorn.

We also never thought that our little girl could go through intense emotional swings and moodiness because of her diet—yet that is what we discovered once we replaced modern wheat with einkorn. All children get tired and have tantrums, but Giulia's emotional outbursts had seemed extreme for such a normally well-behaved child. After eliminating any type of wheat but einkorn, her emotional swings slowly disappeared, and if we allowed her just a small amount of modern wheat, they would return within an hour or two. Even after not

eating wheat for five years, we allowed her to eat a piece of cake at a Connecticut restaurant with a group of friends. After our friends departed, her behavior became extremely annoying, as she complained and nagged us about everything. A few hours later, as we were driving down the street, she started to cry and said, "I feel strange, I am depressed." I could not believe a few bites of cake could do this to her so suddenly and after so many years. It was her younger sister who said what I had been thinking: "It's the wheat, Mom, it's not her fault."

After witnessing our daughter's dramatic improvement, my husband and I knew we had to make einkorn available to others, and I gratefully accepted this as my life's mission. We began growing einkorn near our home in northern Italy and launched jovial, a company devoted to einkorn and gluten-free products. Bringing back einkorn has been both incredibly rewarding and a struggle. Finding seeds, replenishing them for planting, and partnering with farmers who are passionate enough to put up with all of einkorn's challenges is all part of the battle. The beauty of this mission is the discovery that foods made with einkorn taste better.

This book is a celebration of our return to real food, to better health, and to eating foods that are naturally delicious and good for us.

# FROM WILD EINKORN
# TO THE WHEAT OF TODAY

**IN PALEOLITHIC TIMES,** inhabitants of the Fertile Crescent sustained themselves by hunting animals and gathering wild plants. Archaeological evidence shows that these nomadic populations also harvested and consumed cereal grains, including wild einkorn, barley, and rye. Roughly twelve thousand years ago, humans transitioned from Paleolithic hunter-gatherers to Neolithic farmers, which enabled them to become sedentary and to organize their communities around more permanent settlements. The first wild seed that was gathered and planted was einkorn.

Einkorn is of the *Triticum* genus, as are other species of wheat like emmer, spelt, durum, and soft wheat. All wheat is a descendant of wild einkorn, and yet einkorn remains as the original diploid wheat, with only two sets of chromosomes, and the only one never to be hybridized. Hybridization is the crossing of distinctly different species of plants to form a new variety with a new genetic makeup; plant breeding is the science of crossing similar species of plants for what is believed to be improved traits, like higher yields or ease of growing. Emmer appeared about ten thousand years ago through the hybridization of wild einkorn wheat and a wild grass, and is a tetraploid wheat with four sets of chromosomes. Spelt originated in the Near East about five thousand years later through the hybridization of emmer and a wild goat grass, and is a hexaploid wheat with six sets of chromosomes. During the Bronze Age, einkorn was slowly abandoned by farmers for higher-yielding varieties.

Agriculture has changed immensely over the twentieth century. Synthetic nitrogen fertilizers, pesticides, and herbicides were developed for use in farming, and gasoline-powered tractors enabled farms to become large scale. As the world's population exploded, researchers looked for ways to develop agriculture and increase the food supply. During the Green Revolution from the 1940s to the 1960s, breeders created new high-yielding varieties of wheat with hybrid seeds that would carry better traits for large-scale farming. While einkorn, emmer, and spelt grow with a protective layer that covers each grain, modern varieties of wheat grow without the outer husk, making them easier to mill into greater amounts of flour. However, the ancient grains' husks protect the inner seed from mycotoxins, spores of dangerous fungus that develop on the exposed kernels. Genes were mutated to drastically reduce the height of plants so that bending in the wind and rain would not ruin crops. Breeding transformed emmer into today's modern durum wheat, and spelt into today's soft bread wheat, yet einkorn was the only wheat to remain completely untouched. Einkorn's fall in popularity is actually its saving grace—because it survived as a relic grain, its seeds were not selectively harvested or bred for improvements, and it has remained as it was, just as nature intended.

My husband and I heard about einkorn when talking to a researcher who focused on preserving ancient and heritage seeds in Italy. A local group of farmers from northern Italy where einkorn once flourished had been working for a number of years to replenish seeds. We were able to obtain seeds from them and plant a small test crop with a local organic wheat farmer who was up for a challenge. Everything about einkorn was different. We first noticed that the early einkorn wheatgrass was a brilliant bright green, unlike the hunter-green color of modern wheat, and by late July the plants stretched about five feet tall. We noticed how einkorn's tiny grains were attached one seed at a time to the rachis, or shaft, of the plant. In comparison, modern wheat appears supersized and top heavy. We first learned to love the plants in the fields for their noble appearance and were then elated to discover that the tiny wheat berries offered a better flavor as well as superior nutrient content and digestibility.

Ancient einkorn wheat grows with a husk that is removed before the grain is milled to flour.

The evolution of wheat over thousands of years altered the nutrient content of the grain because hybridization changed the size of the kernels. Modern wheat is three times the size of the original einkorn grains. Large seeds have a different ratio of bran, germ, and endosperm. Einkorn contains roughly 30 percent more protein than modern wheat and more protein than any other grain, while having 15 percent less starch, translating to fewer carbohydrates. This increase in protein will leave you feeling more sustained after eating einkorn. It will also change the baking qualities of einkorn flour, which I will discuss further in Working with Einkorn.

| PROTEIN IN EINKORN COMPARED TO OTHER GRAINS (G/100G)* | |
| --- | --- |
| Einkorn | 18.80 |
| Oats | 16.89 |
| Spelt | 14.57 |
| Quinoa | 14.12 |
| Durum wheat | 13.68 |
| Soft wheat | 10.37 |

*Source: USDA National Nutrient Database

Foods that are bred for higher yields and grown on a large scale are less flavorful, because nutrients have flavor, and stretching a plant for greater yield lowers the quantity of nutrients it produces. If you have tasted a tomato picked at the perfect ripeness, you'll notice how that compares to a beautiful but flavorless supermarket tomato. The same is true for wheat, and since einkorn is the lowest-yielding wheat, it is also the most nutritious and flavorful. In fact, einkorn contains 200 percent more lutein than modern wheat, the same antioxidant that gives egg yolks their deep yellow color. When compared to durum wheat, einkorn has 50 percent or more manganese, riboflavin, and zinc and 20 percent or more magnesium, thiamin, niacin, iron, and vitamin B6, all essential nutrients. Ironically, these are the same nutrients that are synthetically added back to enriched wheat flour to compensate for what we've lost by making wheat a high-yield crop.

## WHY EINKORN'S GLUTEN IS DIFFERENT

There is some misunderstanding about einkorn and gluten, with many incorrectly stating that einkorn is better tolerated by the gluten-sensitive because it is lower in gluten. When we refer to protein in certain grains like einkorn, spelt, emmer, barley, rye, durum, and soft wheat, we're actually referring to the proteins that make up gluten. Gluten is a gluey network of proteins that is formed when water and

Einkorn means "one grain" in German because each grain is attached individually, rather than in clusters, to the stalk.

flour are mixed together, which gives dough the ability to hold air bubbles. Since einkorn has more protein than modern wheat, the content of gluten in einkorn is actually similar or even higher than the levels of gluten in modern wheat. However, the reason that gluten in einkorn is different is more significant than simply a question of quantity.

When scientists measure the amount of gluten in flour, they must first mix dough, because dry flour in itself does not contain gluten—instead, it contains groups of proteins called glutenins and gliadins, which bond together to form gluten when mixed with a liquid. Glutenins are further classified as high molecular weight and low molecular weight proteins; modern bread flours are considered of good quality for baking when they have a high content of high molecular weight proteins, which can influence the dough's mixing times, elasticity, and gluten strength—and thus the finished loaf's volume. While einkorn has enough gluten for bread baking, it is lacking in certain high molecular weight proteins, and you can feel how much it differs in its extreme stickiness and reduced elasticity. Gliadins are classified into four groups of protein, and when researchers analyzed the gliadin composition in einkorn, they found that entire groups of γ-gliadins that are present in all other types of wheat are absent in this ancient grain. Einkorn also has a complete imbalance in the ratios of these proteins compared to other wheats, with a much higher ratio of gliadins to glutenins.

So perhaps this is the magic in the supposed flaw of einkorn—when neither of the two gluten-forming proteins behaves as it does in conventional wheat, the gluten in einkorn can be tolerated by many people with sensitivity to wheat, including our own daughter. If you have symptoms of gluten sensitivity and a diagnosis of celiac disease has been ruled out, einkorn may be the only type of wheat you can feel good eating. But once you understand the science behind why einkorn makes you feel so much better, then you can learn how to harness its inherent goodness in delicious breads, baked goods, pasta, and everyday meals.

My mother-in-law, who lived through World War II as a child, tells stories about how different the wheat fields of her youth were. She would snack on the grains right in the field at her family's farm, and her parents baked the week's supply of sourdough bread in a brick oven. I imagine that the flavors and textures of her youth are very similar to what you will be achieving today in your kitchen with ancient einkorn, as you begin your own personal journey to harvest health and wellness from history.

# WORKING WITH
# EINKORN

MANY PEOPLE WOULD LIKE TO CLASSIFY EINKORN as either hard or soft wheat, so they can understand if it is more suitable to making pasta, bread, or sweets. However, einkorn has been around since before wheat was deemed either hard or soft, so you can make every type of recipe successfully with einkorn wheat. Although the final textures may not be the same as when baking with modern wheat, you will quickly taste how much more sustaining and flavorful your food is when made with einkorn. When I bake with einkorn, I challenge myself to work with a fresh mind and not treat the einkorn as an impediment but as an opportunity. You will have tremendous, delicious success with it once you let go of certain standard baking practices. You will actually see and feel the difference in this flour: Silky smooth and golden in color, einkorn flour will reward you with flavorful, wholesome breads and baked goods.

Like other wheat, einkorn can be ground into whole grain or all-purpose flour, meaning a portion of the bran and germ is removed. If you are not a lover of whole grain flours, don't skip out on whole grain einkorn flour just yet. You will find that einkorn whole grain flour does not taste gritty but rather has a sweet and nutty flavor. I like using both all-purpose and whole grain einkorn flour, either on their own or mixed at different ratios, to provide much more variety in my baking. I recommend you keep an open mind toward both flours and learn to use them to your benefit. Einkorn wheat sprouts very easily and can be sprouted, dehydrated, and milled to fresh flour (see page 18). Sprouted flour will add yet another dimension in flavor to your baking, as will homemade rolled einkorn flakes (see page 20), which are a very tasty substitute for old-fashioned oatmeal.

Here are some essential things to consider before you begin baking with einkorn:

- **WHEN MAKING CAKES,** you'll notice that the flour takes longer to fold in, since einkorn absorbs liquid more slowly than other flours. All-purpose einkorn flour is also very fine and can form clumps easily, so it is sometimes a good idea to sift the flour twice before folding it into other ingredients.

- **EINKORN ABSORBS FATS SLOWLY,** so dough that includes fat might seem a bit dry at first, but will soften up after the flour has had time to absorb the fat. Let your piecrusts and cookie dough rest in the refrigerator to give the flour time to absorb the fat fully for a better final texture.

- **OVERMIXING EINKORN WILL ACTIVATE ITS STICKINESS,** so while you can use a standing mixer for all steps prior to adding the flour, it's best to work in the flour by hand unless otherwise indicated.

- **BEATING WHOLE EGGS** on high speed with sugar and then adding them to muffins and cakes can help add lightness to the crumb, which may otherwise seem denser than baked goods made with modern wheat.

- **CAKE AND MUFFIN BATTERS** that are too thin and wet may not firm up completely during baking, so the rule of thumb is to keep batters slightly thicker. It actually takes longer for these types of batters to set in the oven when baking with einkorn, so a hotter oven and stiffer batter will also help added fruits and nuts stay suspended evenly in the finished baked good.

## THE BASICS OF BAKING BREAD WITH EINKORN FLOUR

At first, baking bread with einkorn flour can seem very difficult. If the dough is too dry, the loaf will not rise properly and it will bake up dense, yet if the dough is too wet it will be difficult to handle. Finding the right balance between proper hydration and manageability is the key to success.

You may bake einkorn bread with both active dry yeast and a sourdough starter. Sourdough einkorn bread takes longer to make, but the longer the dough ferments, the better it is for your health and for its flavor. Although yeasted loaves rise faster, you will have to keep a careful eye on the dough while it is proofing—if it proofs too much, the weak gluten in einkorn may not support the rise in the oven, causing the bread to sink during baking. With the selection of the proper cycles, baking in a bread machine (see page 16) will also give you satisfying results.

Here are some bread-baking guidelines to keep in mind while baking from this book:

- The key to good einkorn bread is getting the correct amount of water in the dough. A dough that feels right in your hands will bake dry in the middle because einkorn absorbs water slowly, and what might seem perfect at first will not have enough hydration after a few hours of proofing. Follow the recipes to understand what the right texture should be, and try to refrain from tweaking flour or liquids. Use your hands as much as possible, so you will understand exactly how to gauge the correct consistencies.

- Wetter dough in recipes like Ciabatta (page 45) and Focaccia Genovese (page 48) will promote a better rise and the appearance of large fermentation bubbles in the crumb, but the dough will be very sticky and hard to shape. Drier dough, such as in the Classic French Boule (page 28) and the Whole Grain Batard (page 41), will have a more compact crumb but will be easier to work with. I recommend starting with drier dough until you feel comfortable handling the sticky nature of einkorn, then moving on to the wetter dough.

- The rule of thumb is to let einkorn bread dough rise by half. With some sourdoughs (especially those containing fats or eggs), you will find it takes more time for the dough to rise. You will need to gauge the proofing time based on the temperature and humidity in your kitchen.

- All-purpose and whole grain einkorn flours are not to be substituted cup for cup because whole grain flour will absorb more liquid than the all-purpose flour. To substitute whole grain flour for all-purpose, increase the liquid amount roughly by 5 percent.

- Bread dough that contains oils, eggs, and fats rise slower when made with einkorn flour. I like to cover the dough with oiled plastic wrap to keep the dough moist during proofing. This avoids the formation of a skin, which can further prolong rising.

Here are a few tools I recommend to help you for bread baking with einkorn flour:

- With baking, a **KITCHEN SCALE** is the single most important tool you will need. You will never be able to measure the exact amount of flour needed when measuring with cups, so each recipe includes grams for accuracy. It will be the only way to ensure you are adding the correct amount of flour.

- A **GRAIN MILL** is needed if you wish to grind whole einkorn wheat berries or sprouted and dehydrated wheat berries to flour. While you can use a high-powered blender and grind a cup at a time, the blades will not be able to grind the flour as finely as a grain mill.

- **LARGE, NONMETALLIC MIXING BOWLS** are important in sourdough baking because the higher acidity in the dough can react with metal. I recommend you use glass or earthenware bowls.

- A **STIFF SILICONE SPATULA** can be used to knead most einkorn bread dough or at least get it started so your hands do not have to touch the dough when it is at its stickiest. Once the flour has absorbed the added liquid in the dough, you will be able to handle most types of dough without having it stick to your hands.

- Baking artisan-style loaves in a **DUTCH OVEN**, either enamel-coated or all cast iron, will produce beautiful einkorn bread, as einkorn benefits from high oven temperatures and the extra steam created in the covered pot during baking. You will need a pot with a lid and a minimum 5-quart capacity.

- Because of einkorn's stickiness, it is recommended that you use a **LINEN COUCHE**, a flax linen cloth, when proofing dough that

doesn't use a proofing basket (see next column). Linen is less likely to stick to the dough and it will absorb excess moisture from the surface of the loaf, resulting in a thin and crispy crust after baking. I find that there isn't really a good substitute for a linen couche, so it's worth investing in one if you're going to make einkorn bread on a regular basis.

- **PROOFING BASKETS**, also called banneton baskets, hold the shape of the loaf while proofing. The shaped loaf can be added directly to the well-floured basket, which will produce a beautiful circular design on artisan loaves.

- A **BREAD LAME**, a razor affixed to a long thin plastic handle, is a relatively inexpensive tool used to slash the bread dough before baking, which is important with einkorn bread. Einkorn tends to have a quick spring in the oven and can blow out at weak spots to create an uneven loaf when not slashed properly. You may also use a sharp knife, but sometimes knives can drag through the dough and create a less-than-perfect slash.

- A **DEHYDRATOR** can be used to dry sprouted or soaked wheat berries so that they can be milled to flour or rolled into einkorn flakes. If your oven has a dehydrating setting or can bake at temperatures below 120°F, then you may use your oven.

- **STAINLESS-STEEL SCRUBBING SPONGES**, not to be mistaken for steel wool, are long-lasting thinly intertwined coils of steel that will not rust and are a good tool for removing sticky einkorn dough from your mixing bowl, utensils, and hands.

# CREATING AN EINKORN SOURDOUGH STARTER

Sourdough was accidentally invented by the Egyptians more than five thousand years ago, when a leftover batch of porridge developed into a bubbly, sour-smelling batter that was baked into flatbreads. This accident certainly occurred with einkorn or emmer wheat, so by baking with einkorn sourdough, you are truly going back to the origins of bread.

Studies have shown that the gluten proteins in sourdough bread are broken down during the fermentation process, making the bread easier to digest. Additionally, sourdough bread has a much lower glycemic index than yeasted bread because of the slower rate at which glucose is released into the bloodstream. In fact, in sourdough breads, complex carbohydrates are broken down into simple sugars and protein is broken down into amino acids, while enzymes develop during the fermentation process. Because commercial yeast acts so fast in rising the bread, the same enzymes and probiotics do not have time to act in the same manner.

Einkorn bread made with sourdough starter is also the most flavorful bread you can imagine, and it is made by way of an extremely flexible and foolproof process. The most difficult part is developing your starter—not because it is complicated, but because you might be worried that the starter is not developing, but do not give up. The time it takes for the starter to be ready will differ in every kitchen, and it will take longer if you have never baked bread before. But have faith, and you will be rewarded with the healthiest bread of our ancestors.

I use only einkorn flour, either all-purpose or whole grain, and water to make my starter, though I do also have a recipe for Kefir Sourdough Bread (page 36) that uses fermented milk kefir to jump-start the process. Wild yeasts are naturally present on plants, and in wheat these yeasts live under the thin layer of bran on the wheat kernel. The yeasts remain alive in the flour after milling, and when flour mixed with water is left to rest at room temperature, the mixture will slowly begin to ferment. During this time, the wild yeasts feed on the carbohydrates in the flour and produce lactic acid, or the healthy bacteria known as lactobacillus. (You can detect it in the sweet yogurt smell in your starter.) As the fermentation continues, acetic acid (the same acid found in vinegar) will also be produced, giving your bread a characteristically sour flavor and acting as a natural preservative to help your bread last for many days.

You can control the amount of sourness in your bread by balancing the amount of lactic acid and acetic acid produced during fermentation. Some people really love a strong sour flavor, but in my opinion, the best bread has an overall balanced flavor, like the sourdoughs of France. The longer your dough ferments, the stronger the sour flavor will be. Cooler temperatures also promote the formation of acetic acid, so allowing your dough to proof slowly in the refrigerator will yield a tangy flavor in your bread. My sourdough recipes have a total proofing time that ranges from 4 to 7 hours for the most balanced flavor.

## UNDERSTANDING PROOFING TIMES IN SOURDOUGH BAKING

To a new bread baker, sourdough may seem like a tremendous undertaking because it takes longer for the bread to rise. The beautiful truth about sourdough is that longer proofing times actually free up the baker and can be managed to fit a busy lifestyle better than baking bread with commercial yeast. While einkorn bread made with yeast rises quicker, it can also rise too much, so you will have to keep a close eye on the dough during both the first and second proofing steps. With sourdough einkorn bread, you don't have to worry about overproofing. You can extend the time from a few hours to up to a day; this flexibility is perfect for those with a busy schedule. Longer proofing times will actually produce wonderful bread and you will enjoy the flexibility, especially when you discover you can mix the dough in the evening and enjoy freshly baked bread in the morning.

While you must allow the minimum proofing time indicated in the sourdough bread recipes to pass, you may extend the times as indicated in the following tips:

- Since sourdough and yeast levain must be mixed 6 to 10 hours before baking, you may find at times that your plans to bake bread change once the levain is ready. After the initial proofing at room temperature, you may delay baking and refrigerate the levain for up to 24 hours. When you are ready to proceed the next day, remove the levain from the refrigerator, even if the bubbling has subsided a bit, and continue with the recipe.

- When baking bread with sourdough or yeast levain, you may extend the first proofing time of 3 to 5 hours, meaning you may leave the dough out to rise for up to 8 hours at room temperature or up to 20 hours by placing the dough in the refrigerator. Longer proofing times at room temperature can increase the sour flavor of the bread. The cool temperatures will retard or slow down the fermentation process and you will often find that einkorn bread tastes even better with this type of slower fermentation.

- If you start the first proofing time at room temperature and you want to delay baking, you can still place the dough in the refrigerator to extend the proofing time until you are ready to bake.

- If a recipe includes turning the dough, you should not skip that step even if you plan on letting the dough rise in the refrigerator for many hours.

- The one step of sourdough bread baking that cannot be delayed is the final proofing time after shaping. Therefore, while you may lengthen the first proof to fit your schedule, once you remove the dough from the refrigerator and shape your bread, you must follow the times indicated in the recipes for the final proofing before the bread is baked.

# EINKORN SOURDOUGH STARTER

It will normally take 6 to 10 days to get your starter strong enough to bake great bread. At that point, the starter may be stored in the refrigerator and refreshed just once a week. You can create and maintain the starter with either all-purpose or whole grain einkorn flour. The whole grain flour contains 100 percent of the seed and a bit more of the wild yeasts, which can help things to move along quicker in the beginning, but both flours will end up working equally as well.

MAKES 1 CUP OF STARTER

**TO BEGIN THE STARTER**

3 tablespoons (45 g) warm water, at 100°F

½ cup (60 g) all-purpose einkorn flour or ½ cup (48 g) whole grain einkorn flour, plus more for dusting

(A) In a small bowl, mix together the water and flour with a fork to form a wet dough. (B) Dust your hands lightly with flour, scrape up the dough, and roll gently between your hands into a sticky ball without adding more flour. (C) Transfer to a sealable glass jar or container, or simply leave it in the bowl and tightly seal with plastic wrap. Store the bowl in a dark place for 48 hours where it is at least 68°F.

**TO FEED THE STARTER**

2 tablespoons (30 g) warm water, at 100°F

½ cup (60 g) all-purpose einkorn flour or ½ cup (48 g) whole grain einkorn flour, plus more for dusting

After 48 hours of resting, the starter should smell sharp and have expanded minimally, with bubbles visible under the pale gray surface of the dough. (D) With a fork, gently push aside and discard the gray surface of the dough. (E) Gather up the remaining starter and transfer it to another medium bowl. Add the water and mix until the mixture is smooth and creamy. Add the flour and mix until a wet dough is formed.

Dust your hands lightly with flour, scrape up the dough, and roll gently between your hands into a sticky ball without adding more flour. Transfer to a clean and dry sealable glass jar or container or to a clean bowl and tightly seal with plastic wrap. Store in a dark place for 24 hours where it is at least 68°F. (Some say you should cover the container with a cotton towel so the starter is able to catch wild yeasts in your kitchen. However, all of the wild yeast you need is already in the flour, and the added air can form a skin on the surface of the starter.)

## TO FEED AND FINISH THE STARTER

2 tablespoons (30 g) warm water

½ cup (60 g) all-purpose einkorn flour or ½ cup (48 g) whole grain einkorn flour, plus more for dusting

After the fed starter has rested 24 hours, it should begin to change from a sharp to a sweeter, yogurtlike smell. You should begin to see bubbles not only under the surface of the dough, but also on top. **(F)** If you still see hooch, a grayish hue on the surface of the starter, push it aside with a fork and discard it. Add the water and mix until the mixture is smooth and creamy. Add the flour and mix until a wet dough is formed. Dust your hands lightly with flour, scrape up the dough, and roll gently with your hands into a sticky ball without adding more flour. Transfer to a clean and dry sealable glass jar or container or simply transfer to a new bowl and tightly seal with plastic wrap. Store in a dark place for 24 hours where it is at least 68°F.

After this final 24 hours, you may bake with the starter, but it will not be as mature as the starter used in my recipes. **(G)** Therefore, the proofing times will need to be increased from 3 to 5 hours to 12 to 15 hours, or your bread may bake dense until you have the proper balance of acids. I recommend strengthening your starter even further before you mix your first loaf of bread. To do this, you should refresh your starter (see page 13) at least 5 times until it bubbles up and subsides in less than 5 hours after each refreshing. You can still bake great bread while your starter is maturing, by using Yeast Levain (page 14) and mixing in the excess starter you have each time you refresh.

(continues)

| DAY 1 | DAY 3 | DAY 4 | DAY 5 | DAYS 6–10 |
|---|---|---|---|---|
| Begin the Starter | Feed the Starter | Finish the Starter | Refresh the Starter | Refresh the Starter |
| Mix the flour and water. Cover and let rest for 2 days. | Mix starter from Day 1 with flour and water. Cover and let rest for 24 hours. | Mix starter from Day 3 with flour and water. Cover and let rest for 24 hours. | Mix starter from Day 4 with flour and water. Cover and let rest for 6 to 12 hours. | Refresh twice per day until the starter bubbles up within 5 hours of refreshing. Bake bread. |

Creating your very own sourdough starter and discovering how your bread rises and tastes is an extraordinary experience.

The way you will refresh your starter from Day 6 forward is how you will do it forever. When you first begin, your starter will not have the correct pH to thrive, but this will develop over time with multiple refreshing. It may seem terrible to throw away what you have made so far, but it would be more wasteful to keep refreshing large amounts of starter and not using them for baking bread. Therefore, you will take just 2 teaspoons (10 g) of your previous batch each time you refresh, and discard the rest. For each baker, the time it will take to get your starter active is different. Weighing each ingredient with a baking scale will help prevent many problems.

When your starter bubbles up within 6 to 10 hours of refreshing, you are ready to bake bread. When you are baking bread and the dough is rising nicely in 3 to 5 hours as recommended in the recipes, you can refrigerate your starter and refresh it one time per week. You will not discard starter anymore, but rather use your starter to bake bread until it runs low, then refresh it to replenish your supply. I've given you two recipes for refreshing, and they are based on how many loaves of bread you will normally make in a week. If you are away for a few weeks, your starter will survive just fine if stored in a sealed container in the refrigerator.

## REFRESHING YOUR STARTER

**makes about ⅓ cup (100 g), enough for 3 loaves of bread per week**

2 teaspoons (10 g) Einkorn Sourdough Starter (page 10)

2 tablespoons (30 g) warm water, at 100°F

½ cup (60 g) all-purpose einkorn flour or ½ cup (48 g) whole grain einkorn flour

**makes about ⅔ cup (165 g), enough for 5 or 6 loaves of bread per week**

4 teaspoons (20 g) Einkorn Sourdough Starter (page 10)

¼ cup (56 g) warm water, at 100°F

¾ cup plus 1 tablespoon (100 g) all-purpose einkorn flour or ¾ cup plus 1 tablespoon (90 g) whole grain einkorn flour

Place the starter in a small bowl. Add the water and mix with a fork until the mixture is smooth and creamy. Add the flour and knead to form a firm ball. Roll the starter between your hands until the flour is absorbed; add a tiny bit more if it seems overly sticky, but the dough should remain very moist. Store in a large sealed container (so you have room for the starter to expand) for 6 to 12 hours. The starter will bubble up and then subside. Refrigerate the starter until you refresh it again. Remember to always leave your einkorn starter in a dark place because light can oxidize the carotenoids in the flour.

To bake bread, you will remove a small piece of the starter to mix a sourdough levain the night before baking. Some recipes will also call for kneading the dough straight with the starter. Remember to monitor the amount of sourdough that remains, because you will always need to have at least 2 teaspoons (10 g) for refreshing. The original starter you create can survive forever, so make a note of when you begin so you'll know how old your starter is as the years pass.

## BAKING WITH LEVAIN (FOR SOURDOUGH AND YEAST BREADS)

The majority of bread recipes in this book use a pre-ferment to leaven the dough. Levain is a wet, batterlike dough made with a small quantity of yeast or sourdough starter, water, and flour that is mixed and allowed to slowly ferment prior to mixing the dough on the day of baking. This extra step will yield the best tasting and most easily digested einkorn bread. In the case of sourdough bread, this step will significantly shorten the proofing times. Compared with breads made with dry active yeast, it will enable you to reduce the yeast to a minimum so your bread will proof slower, taste much better, and stay fresh longer.

# SOURDOUGH LEVAIN

makes 1 cup (280 g)

2 tablespoons (30 g) Einkorn Sourdough Starter (page 10)

½ cup plus 1 tablespoon (130 g) warm water, at 100°F

1 cup (120 g) all-purpose einkorn flour or 1¼ cups (120 g) whole grain einkorn flour

In a medium bowl, mix the starter and water together until the mixture is smooth and creamy. Mix in the flour with a fork until all of the flour is absorbed. Cover and let stand at room temperature for 6 to 10 hours. (A) The levain is ready to use when the surface of the mixture is covered with large bubbles. However, if you mix a batch of sourdough levain and then decide you want to delay baking, you may refrigerate the levain for up to 24 hours and then use it the next day.

# YEAST LEVAIN

makes 1 cup (250 g)

Pinch of dry active yeast, plus ¼ teaspoon

½ cup plus 1 tablespoon (130 g) warm water, at 100°F

1 cup (120 g) all-purpose einkorn flour or 1¼ cups (120 g) whole grain einkorn flour

In a medium bowl, mix a small pinch of yeast and water together until the yeast dissolves. Mix in the flour until combined. Cover and let stand at room temperature for 6 to 8 hours. (A) The levain is ready to use when the surface of the mixture is covered with large bubbles. Just before mixing your dough on the day of baking, mix in the remaining ¼ teaspoon of yeast to ensure that your bread rises properly. This additional yeast will not be listed in the recipe, so don't forget this last step.

## TURNING THE DOUGH

All einkorn bread dough is essentially no-knead because it is normally too wet to knead thoroughly in a standing mixer and the powerful mixing will only make the dough stickier. Because einkorn is slow to absorb liquids, your bread dough will be rather wet and sticky when you first mix it. Turning the dough is a technique used by professional bakers and also an essential step in baking the best einkorn bread, especially breads with shorter proofing times.

Turning the dough 1 to 3 times in the first hour after mixing the dough will firm up the wet dough and help develop the gluten in the flour. Because turning adds more flour to the dough, the recipes that include turning may be too wet and sticky for shaping if this step is not followed. (If you decide to skip the turning step, add 2 tablespoons of flour per turn to the recipe.) You can see for yourself how turning works by placing a ball of freshly mixed dough on the counter. At first, you will see that the dough quickly sags and expands. With each turn and resting period, the dough will spring up and hold its shape better.

Turning the dough is an essential step in baking great einkorn bread because the process helps to strengthen einkorn's weak gluten.

(continues)

To turn the dough, scrape the dough out of the bowl with your hands or with the help of a bowl scraper. Lightly flour a work surface and place the dough on it. Dust the top of the dough with flour, and use your hands to gently spread the dough out to a rectangle that is about 1 inch thick—be careful to stretch, not punch down, the dough. (B-D) Starting from the left side, fold each side of the rectangle to the center, working your way along the four sides. You should have a square consisting of 4 layers of folded dough. (E) Fold the square in half, gather up the dough with your hands, and place it back in the bowl. Cover the bowl as indicated in the recipe and let the dough rest for a minimum of 15 minutes between each turn (the recipe's proofing time begins once you have finished the last turn).

## BAKING IN A BREAD MACHINE

All of the sandwich loaf recipes in this book may be baked in a bread machine. The key to success with baking einkorn bread in a machine is to use the correct cycle or create custom cycles. Other recipes can also be baked in the machine, as long as they do not exceed the capacity of your machine.

Einkorn dough is very sticky and can adhere to the sides of the pan when the machine is kneading, leading to a lopsided loaf. Since the kneading time with einkorn bread is very short, you should wait until the first knead is complete and scrape down the sides of the pan if the dough has adhered to them.

**FOR YEASTED LOAVES:** Add all of the liquids and fats called for in the recipe to the baking pan first. If the recipe calls for eggs, beat them in a small bowl and add them to the liquids along with the salt and the sweetener. Add the flour on top. Make a depression in the middle of the flour and add the yeast. Set the crust to dark. For yeasted loaves, you should set a custom cycle on your machine as follows: Preheat off, Knead 10 minutes, Rise 1: 30 minutes, Rise 2: 30 minutes, Rise 3: off, Bake (follow baking time in the recipe), Keep Warm off. (If you are unable to add a custom cycle, select the shortest cycle on your machine.)

**FOR SOURDOUGH LOAVES:** Add all of the liquid, sourdough starter, or sourdough or yeasted levain, and fats and sweeteners to the baking pan first. If the recipe calls for eggs, beat them in a small bowl and add them to the liquids. Add flour and salt as called for in the recipe on top of the liquids. Set the crust to dark and bake with a custom cycle set as follows for a 5-hour cycle: Preheat off, Knead 10 minutes, Rise 1: 1 hour, Rise 2: 2 hours, Rise 3: 1 hour, Bake (follow baking time in the recipe), Keep Warm off. (If you are unable to add a custom cycle with your machine, select the cycle with the longest proofing times.)

## THE BASICS OF WORKING WITH EINKORN WHEAT BERRIES

Once we started to grow einkorn with a local farmer, we wanted to discover more about the history of the grain. We visited the South Tyrol Museum of Archaeology in Bolzano, Italy, to see Ötzi the Iceman, the Bronze Age man who had been perfectly preserved in ice for five thousand years, and who had eaten whole wheat berries at his last meal. The museum displays the einkorn seeds that were found on the fur of Ötzi's coat, and they look amazingly as fresh as the wheat berries you will be using in your kitchen today.

Stocking your pantry with einkorn wheat berries will give you a whole grain flour that is packed with a healthy abundance of plant protein and fiber in each serving. Whole wheat berries can be soaked and cooked whole like brown rice or cracked or ground coarse for porridge and polenta. If you have a grain mill or grain flaker, you can also transform the whole grains to fresh or sprouted whole grain flour or rolled grains similar to old-fashioned oats. Einkorn grains are very fast to sprout, and the whole sprouted grains can be steamed for salads or dehydrated and ground to flour.

Einkorn plants all start out as green grass, and when the plants go to seed in the hot summer, the seeds or wheat kernels are harvested and milled to produce flour. Einkorn seeds have a protective husk around them when harvested, and this layer is removed before being sold as a whole wheat berry or milled to flour. When a grain sprouts, its enzymes, amino acids, and certain B vitamins are known to increase, while starch and phytic acid decrease. The digestibility of protein and starch are also improved. You can sprout grains at home and either cook them whole or slowly dry them at lower temperatures to produce sprouted flour. Sprouted einkorn wheat berries have a complex and enjoyable lightly malted flavor. For me, sprouted einkorn berries add another great ingredient to my kitchen, which I can use occasionally to pleasantly alter the flavor of my baking and cooking.

# SPROUTED EINKORN WHEAT BERRIES

The process for sprouting can vary from 15 to 48 hours. Once the berries start to sprout, it's important to stop the sprouting process to prevent bacteria from forming. (Also, the texture of baked goods made with oversprouted grains will be gummy, so you have a small window to produce your ideal sprouts.) I do not recommend using a sprouting jar for einkorn because the pressure of too many grains stacked on top of one another can inhibit the sprouting process because the kernels are small and soft. All you need is a large bowl and a fine mesh strainer or colander. MAKES 4 CUPS (800 G) OF SPROUTED EINKORN WHEAT BERRIES, OR ABOUT 8 CUPS (800 G) OF WHOLE GRAIN SPROUTED EINKORN FLOUR

4 cups (800 g) einkorn wheat berries

TO SPROUT THE WHEAT BERRIES: Place the wheat berries in a large bowl. Add enough water to cover the wheat berries by 2 to 3 inches. Let them soak for 12 hours.

Transfer the wheat berries to a fine mesh strainer or colander.

If the wheat berries haven't started sprouting, rinse them gently with clean water and let them drain. Once the water has drained well, place the filled strainer or colander over a large bowl. Place the bowl near an area of natural light but not direct sunshine. In the winter months, rinse the berries twice per day, draining well before placing the strainer on top of the bowl. In the summer months, they will dry out quicker and this can inhibit sprouting, so keep them just damp by rinsing 3 or 4 times per day. In less than 24 hours, you should see a small white sprout emerge from one end of the grain. Do not let the sprouts grow longer than $\frac{1}{8}$ inch in length.

**TO DRY THE WHEAT BERRIES:** Place the grains on a baking sheet in the oven for 5 hours; if you have a dehydrating cycle, the temperature should be set no higher than 120°F. If your oven temperature cannot be set that low, you must dry the grains in a dehydrator at 115°F for 5 hours. Drying at higher temperatures will give the wheat berries an off-flavor.

The amount of drying should return the wheat berries to their original moisture level before soaking, and, therefore, when they are ground in a grain mill to sprouted flour, the flour may be substituted 1:1 in all recipes calling for whole grain einkorn flour; but, depending on the level of moisture achieved after dehydrating, you may have to adjust the liquids in the recipe slightly. This time may vary depending on the method you use to dehydrate the wheat berries, so weigh the wheat berries before soaking and after drying and adjust the time until you can get as close as possible to the same weight.

# FLAKING EINKORN WHEAT BERRIES

We are all familiar with rolled oats—whole oat groats are steamed and pressed into old-fashioned oatmeal. In Europe, many grains like rye, spelt, and barley are also flaked and used in muesli. Flaked einkorn can be used in the place of oats when preparing breakfast porridge, high-protein granola, or in breads, cookies, and quick breads. Einkorn flakes are very flavorful and have more protein than oats, so they make a nice substitute in any recipe that calls for oatmeal.

MAKES 4½ CUPS (400 G) ROLLED EINKORN FLAKES

**2 cups (400 g) einkorn wheat berries**

To prepare the wheat berries for flaking, add the wheat berries to a medium bowl and cover with 3 cups (708 g) water. Soak for 12 hours and then dehydrate them, just as you do with the sprouting process, but reduce the drying time to 4 hours (see page 18). Add 1 cup of dehydrated einkorn wheat berries to a grain flaker and begin to crank the machine. Stop to tighten or loosen the rollers so the flakes come out flat but do not break up.

If you would like to make sprouted flaked einkorn, you will follow the instructions in the sprouting process until you have the dehydrated grains. Press the dried wheat berries through the flaker to create rolled einkorn. Einkorn is very small, so expect some breakage during rolling.

## STORING EINKORN FLOUR AND WHEAT BERRIES

Whole grains and flours are delicate items that should be stored properly to maintain integrity and freshness. The most prudent step to proper storage is estimating and storing only what you will be using over a 1- to 2-month period of time and not opening more than that amount. Therefore, if you bake infrequently, it is not a good idea to buy a bulk amount of whole grain flour for savings, because that product is delicate. It's best to buy smaller amounts more frequently and then always work with the freshest ingredients. Here is how you can store all of your einkorn ingredients for maximum freshness:

- All-purpose einkorn flour has a portion of the bran and germ removed after milling and is the most shelf-stable type of einkorn flour. It may be stored at room temperature away from direct sunlight or sources of heat for 90 days. For longer storage or if the temperatures in your kitchen are frequently above 75°F, refrigeration or freezing in an airtight container is recommended.

- Whole grain einkorn flour may be stored at room temperature away from direct sunlight or sources of heat for up to 30 days. For longer storage or if the temperatures in your kitchen are frequently above 75°F, refrigeration or freezing in an airtight container is recommended.

- If einkorn wheat berries are packaged in an airtight bag, they will stay fresh until the expiration date indicated on the package. Once opened, wheat berries can be stored at room temperature in an airtight container away from direct sunlight or sources of heat for 60 days. For longer storage or if the temperatures in your kitchen are frequently above 75°F, refrigeration in an airtight container is recommended.

- Sprouted einkorn wheat berries that have been properly dehydrated may be stored at room temperature away from direct sunlight or sources of heat for up to 30 days. For longer storage or if the temperatures in your kitchen are frequently above 75°F, refrigeration in an airtight container is recommended. Once the sprouted grain is ground to flour, follow the recommendations for whole grain einkorn flour.

- Rolled einkorn flakes may be stored at room temperature away from direct sunlight or sources of heat for up to 30 days. For longer storage or if the temperatures in your kitchen are frequently above 75°F, refrigeration in an airtight container is recommended.

# BREADS
## & CRACKERS

DAIRY-FREE BROWN BREAD

TWO-HOUR DAIRY-FREE
SANDWICH LOAF

CLASSIC FRENCH BOULE

NO-KNEAD OVERNIGHT
ARTISAN LOAF

SEMI-WHOLE GRAIN EINKORN
BREAD RING

FRENCH BAGUETTES

KEFIR SOURDOUGH BREAD

CLASSIC SANDWICH LOAF

WHOLE WHEAT
SANDWICH LOAF

WHOLE GRAIN BATARD

RAISIN AND WALNUT MICHE

CIABATTA

SPROUTED COUNTRY LOAF

FOCACCIA GENOVESE

TOMATO AND ROSEMARY
WHOLE GRAIN FOCACCIA
ROUNDS

PANE TOSCANO

SEMI-WHOLE GRAIN
KAISER ROLLS

BRAIDED EGG BREAD

EINKORN CORN BREAD

BAGELS

SWEET POTATO ROLLS

HAMBURGER AND
HOT DOG BUNS

PITA BREAD

DELI-STYLE EINKORN
RYE BREAD

FLOUR TORTILLAS

THIN GRISSINI

SEA SALT CRACKERS

PARMIGIANO-REGGIANO
CHEESE CRACKERS

WHOLE WHEAT THINS

Kefir Sourdough Bread, page 36

**THE TASTE OF THE FIRST EINKORN SOURDOUGH LOAVES** I baked was fine, but the texture was very dense and dry, and I'd never serve those loaves to friends or family at a dinner party. Soon I learned that minimal hand mixing and wetter dough improved the quality of my bread immensely. As a busy mom, I was delighted to discover that the less I kneaded and fussed with the dough, the better the bread baked up.

Einkorn absorbs water slowly and feels very sticky at first, but it's still a good idea to work with your hands so you can understand when you have obtained the right consistency. Sticky dough is difficult to handle, but you can use a stiff silicone spatula for most of the kneading and a bowl scraper to remove the dough from the bowl to help with shaping. You will first mix up rough, shaggy dough, let the dough rest briefly, remove it from the bowl, and then fold it a number of times. This process will promote a better rise and give more structure to your bread.

When proofing einkorn bread made with active dry yeast, keep in mind that the dough should not rise more than 50 percent, or it will overproof and collapse in the oven because the wheat's gluten will not be strong enough to hold in the bubbles that have formed. Einkorn sourdough bread can rise more than 50 percent during the first proofing, but keep an eye on the second proofing once the loaf is formed. Overproofing after shaping will limit the amount of spring the bread gets in the hot oven and produce a pitted crust that is not firm and crisp.

And, of course, it is hard to resist slicing into that warm loaf of bread right when you pull it out of the oven. However, the inside of the loaf is still cooking while cooling, and slicing the loaf while it is hot can result in an undercooked and gummy crumb. So let your breads cool completely before slicing—then you can relax and enjoy your daily einkorn bread!

BROWN BREAD CAN BE made in many different ways—with mostly whole grain wheat or rye flour, with molasses or maple syrup, and with baking soda or yeast. My recipe is very simple and will only take two hours to prepare, from start to finish. I found that the best texture for this type of loaf comes from a mix of 55 percent whole grain and 45 percent all-purpose einkorn flour. The dough will seem very wet at first, but the bread will shape nicely and bake up soft and delicious.

MAKES 1 LOAF

# DAIRY-FREE BROWN BREAD

1⅓ cups (315 g) warm water, at 100°F

1½ teaspoons active dry yeast

1 tablespoon pure maple syrup

3 tablespoons extra-virgin olive oil or coconut oil, plus more for greasing the pan

3 cups (288g) whole grain einkorn flour

2 cups (240g) all-purpose einkorn flour, plus more for dusting

½ teaspoon fine sea salt

1 In a small bowl, mix together the water, yeast, maple syrup, and oil. In a large bowl, combine the flour and salt. Add the yeast mixture to the flour mixture, and stir the dough with a stiff spatula until all of the flour is absorbed. (You may need to use your hands to incorporate all of the flour.) Cover the bowl with plastic wrap and let stand for 45 minutes. Generously grease an 8½ × 4½-inch loaf pan.

2 Lightly flour a work surface. Scrape the dough out of the bowl and transfer it to the work area. Spread out the dough by pulling gently on the edges to form a 10-inch-long oval. Pull up each corner and tuck tightly in the center to form a rectangle. Flip over and roll the rectangle back and forth until the bottom begins to stick to the work

surface, which will close the seam. Place the loaf seam side down into the pan. Cover the pan with lightly oiled plastic wrap and let proof for 30 minutes—when the center of the loaf rises enough to touch the plastic wrap and the surface of the dough shows the first bubbles, it is ready to bake. (During hot summer months, this second proofing may take less than 30 minutes.) Preheat the oven to 425°F.

3 Lower the heat to 375°F and bake the loaf for 40 minutes until browned on top. Let the loaf cool in the pan for 15 minutes, then turn it out onto a cooling rack. Turn the loaf over and let cool for 2 hours before slicing. If you like very soft bread, drape a clean kitchen towel on top of the loaf so the bread absorbs the steam and the crust softens. Store in a sealed plastic bag for up to 2 days, or freeze for up to 1 month.

**WITH THIS STRAIGHTFORWARD RECIPE,** you can have freshly baked einkorn bread in about 2 hours from start to finish. Once you form the loaf, it will only fill the loaf pan halfway, but you will see it spring up nicely in the hot oven. You may substitute any type of fat for the oil, and if you prefer honey or maple syrup in place of sugar, reduce the total amount of sweetener to 1 tablespoon. MAKES 1 LOAF

# TWO-HOUR DAIRY-FREE SANDWICH LOAF

1¼ cups (295 g) warm water, at 100°F

1½ teaspoons active dry yeast

2 tablespoons sugar

2 tablespoons oil

3¾ cups (450 g) all-purpose einkorn flour, plus more for dusting

1¼ teaspoons fine sea salt

1  In a small bowl, combine the water, yeast, sugar, and oil. In a large bowl, combine the flour and salt. Stir the yeast mixture into the flour with a stiff spatula until all of the flour is absorbed. Cover the bowl with plastic wrap and let stand for 45 minutes. Generously grease an 8½ × 4½-inch loaf pan.

2  Heavily flour a work surface. Scrape the dough out of the bowl and transfer it to the work area. (The dough will be quite wet, so you will need to add a few tablespoons of flour to work with it.) Knead the dough a few times, then spread out the dough by pulling gently on the edges to form an 8-inch-long oval. Fold the oval into thirds like a letter, lifting and pressing the ends to the center.

Stretch, fold, and press the top and bottom into the center to form a loaf shape. Place the dough in the prepared loaf pan, then cover the pan with lightly oiled plastic wrap and let proof at room temperature for 30 minutes, or until the top of the loaf reaches the edges of the loaf pan. Preheat the oven to 425°F.

3  Lower the heat to 375°F and bake the bread for 40 minutes until browned on top. Let the loaf cool in the pan for 15 minutes, then turn out the loaf onto a cooling rack. Let the loaf cool for 2 hours before slicing. If you like very soft bread, drape a clean kitchen towel on top of the loaf so the steam is absorbed and the crust softens. Store in a sealed plastic bag for up to 2 days, or freeze for up to 1 month.

AFTER DISCOVERING THAT MY daughter could eat einkorn, I quickly invested in a standing mixer because I knew I would be baking all of our family's bread from that moment forward. It took me quite a while to get my sourdough starter perfect, to understand the right ratios of einkorn flour to water, and to get used to the gluey batter that stuck to the sides of the mixer. While on vacation without the mixer, I hurriedly threw together this recipe. The batter was too dry to finish mixing with a wooden spoon, so I added extra water so I could finish mixing the dough without getting my hands sticky. That's when I discovered that extra water and quick mixing makes the best einkorn bread and that all einkorn bread is essentially no-knead. MAKES ONE 8-INCH ROUND LOAF

# CLASSIC FRENCH BOULE

5 cups (600 g) all-purpose einkorn flour, plus more for dusting

1½ teaspoons fine sea salt

1 batch Sourdough Levain (page 14) or Yeast Levain (page 14)

1⅓ cups (315 g) warm water, at 100°F

**1** In a large bowl, mix together the flour and salt. Set the levain in a medium bowl. Add the water to the levain and stir to combine before pouring it into the bowl with the flour. Mix the ingredients with a stiff spatula as much as you can until you have a wet, sticky dough. Cover the bowl with a plate and let stand for 15 minutes.

**2** Scrape around the edges of the bowl to loosen the dough. Lightly flour a work surface and transfer the dough to it. Knead the dough until smooth, about 2 minutes, using a dough scraper to help handle the dough if it's sticky. Turn the dough (see page 15) 3 times at 15-minute intervals. After the last turn, cover the bowl and let proof for 3 to 5 hours.

**3** Scrape the dough from the bowl and turn it out onto a lightly floured surface. Knead the dough a number of times until just smooth and form it into a round ball. Flip over the ball and stretch out the edges to form a 10-inch-long oval. Pull up each corner and the middle of each side, pressing them tightly into the center, to make a 6-inch round. Turn the dough over so the seam side is on the counter. Cup the dough with both hands and rotate in a circular motion between your hands until you have a tight round loaf. Dust the top of the loaf generously with flour.

**4** Heavily dust an 8½-inch unlined proofing basket with flour and invert the loaf into it. Cover with a linen couche or plastic wrap and let proof at room temperature for 60 to 90 minutes.

**5** Place a Dutch oven with the lid on in the oven. Preheat the oven to 500°F for 30 minutes.

**6** Remove the pot from the oven and take off the lid. Invert the loaf and place it in the pot seam side down. Cut four ½-inch-deep slashes in the top of the loaf. Cover and place in the oven.

**7** Reduce the oven temperature to 450°F and bake for 40 minutes. At this point, you can remove the pot from the oven and take off the lid. If you like your loaf darker, return the uncovered pot to the oven for 5 minutes.

**8** Lift the loaf out of the pot with oven mitts. Place on a wire rack to cool for 2 hours before slicing. Wrap the loaf in a clean cotton or linen kitchen towel for up to 3 days, or freeze in a sealed plastic bag for up to 1 month.

FOR THOSE NEW TO bread baking, this is a recipe you should try first because it requires no kneading or shaping skills and yet it looks like it came from an artisan bakery. The only catch is that you really need a 5- to 7-quart Dutch oven for baking. Simply mix together the ingredients in the evening before you go to bed. In the morning, you will fold the dough into a rough round, and your fresh loaf will be out of the oven in less than an hour. MAKES ONE 8-INCH ROUND LOAF

# NO-KNEAD OVERNIGHT ARTISAN LOAF

2 cups (472 g) warm water, at 100°F

¼ cup (60 g) refreshed Einkorn Sourdough Starter (page 13) or ¼ teaspoon active dry yeast

6 cups (720 g) all-purpose einkorn flour, or 7¼ cups (696 g) whole grain einkorn flour, plus more for dusting

1½ teaspoons fine sea salt

1 In a large bowl, mix together the water and yeast or starter until dissolved and creamy. Add the flour and salt and mix until all of the flour is absorbed and you have a sticky dough. Cover the bowl with plastic wrap and let rise in a dark place for 10 to 15 hours until the dough has doubled in size.

2 Generously flour a work surface and transfer the dough to it. Use a dough scraper to fold the dough in thirds, dusting with flour as you go, then cup the dough with both hands and rotate in a circular motion between your hands until you have a tight, round loaf. Dust the top of the dough generously with flour.

3 Place a linen couche in a colander, heavily dusted with flour. Place the loaf seam side up in the colander, then fold over the linen to cover. Let proof at room temperature for 30 minutes.

4 Place a Dutch oven with the lid on in the oven. Preheat the oven to 500°F for 30 minutes.

5 Remove the pot from the oven and take off the lid. Invert the loaf and place it in the pot seam side down. Shake to center it, but if it sticks to the side leave it. Cover and place in the oven.

6 Reduce the oven temperature to 450°F and bake for 40 minutes. At this point, you can remove the pot from the oven and take off the lid. If you like your loaf darker, return the uncovered pot to the oven for 5 minutes.

7 Lift the loaf out of the pot with oven mitts. Place on a wire rack to cool for 2 hours before slicing. Wrap the loaf in a clean cotton or linen kitchen towel for up to 3 days, or freeze in a sealed plastic bag for up to 1 month.

**THIS OLD-FASHIONED STYLE OATMEAL** bread is made new and delicious with rolled einkorn flakes and a nice mix of both all-purpose and whole grain flour. Rather than using a yeast levain, this loaf is made with straight yeast or sourdough starter. Avoid overproofing the shaped loaf—it should not have excessive pitting or bubbling on the surface of the dough before you bake it. For direct sourdough, the proofing times will be much longer than when using the levain, so this is a great bread to prepare before going to bed and bake in the morning. MAKES ONE 10-INCH RING-SHAPED LOAF

# SEMI-WHOLE GRAIN EINKORN BREAD RING

1 cup plus 2 tablespoons (95 g) rolled einkorn flakes or old-fashioned rolled oats

1 cup (236 g) boiling water

¾ cup (183 g) whole milk

1 tablespoon pure maple syrup

¼ cup (60 g) refreshed Einkorn Sourdough Starter (page 13) or 1½ teaspoons active dry yeast

2½ cups (300 g) all-purpose einkorn flour, plus more for dusting

2½ cups (240 g) whole grain einkorn flour

1½ teaspoons fine sea salt

4 tablespoons (56 g) unsalted butter, melted and cooled

**1** Add 1 cup (90 g) einkorn flakes to a large bowl. Stir in the water and let stand for 15 minutes. Add the milk, maple syrup, and starter or yeast.

**2** In a medium bowl, mix together the flours and salt. Add the liquid mixture to the flour and combine with a stiff spatula as much as you can. Stir in the butter and then knead in the bowl with your hands until the dough holds just together. Cover the bowl with a plate and let stand for 15 minutes.

**3** Lightly flour a work surface and transfer the dough to it. Knead the dough for 1 minute until it goes from sticky to more compact. When the dough begins to stick to the counter, place it back in the bowl and seal tightly with plastic wrap. If using yeast, let rest for 45 minutes. If using sourdough, let rest for 8 to 10 hours at room temperature, or for up to 15 hours in the refrigerator.

**4** Lightly flour a work surface. Remove the dough from the bowl and turn it out onto the work area. Knead the dough a number of times until smooth and then form a rough ball. Flip over the ball and stretch out the edges to form a 10-inch-long oval. Pull up each corner and the middle of each side, and press them tightly into the center to form a 6-inch round. Turn the dough over so the seam side is on the counter. Rotate the dough in a circular motion between cupped hands until you have a tight round loaf.

**5** Line a baking sheet with parchment paper. Place the loaf in the center of the sheet, seam side down. Use your index and middle fingers to pull out a hole in the center of the loaf all the way to the pan. Enlarge the hole with your hands until it is about 4 inches in diameter. Sprinkle the remaining 2 tablespoons of einkorn flakes over the top of the loaf; press gently to help them stick. Cover the loaf with oiled plastic wrap. If using yeast, let rest for 30 minutes. If using sourdough starter, let rest for 90 minutes.

**6** Preheat the oven to 400°F. Place the baking sheet in the oven bake the loaf for 40 minutes until lightly golden. Cool on the baking sheet for 2 hours before slicing. Store in a sealed plastic bag for up to 3 days, or freeze for up to 1 month.

A GOOD FRENCH BAGUETTE is all about the crust, not the crumb. Roll these loaves out long and thin and don't be afraid to extend the baking time—even when the loaves look done, leave them in the oven for an extra 5 minutes. This extra time will give you that deep brown *bien-cuit* crust that will crackle in your mouth. What differs in this recipe from the other recipes using sourdough or yeast levain is the first step of preparing *pâte fermentée,* a small portion of dough that is mixed and allowed to rise, then incorporated in the full batch on the day of baking. If you proof the dough in the refrigerator rather than at room temperature, it will be much easier to shape the dough, and the flavor will be even more authentic. MAKES 3 BAGUETTES

# FRENCH BAGUETTES

FOR THE PÂTE FERMENTÉE

¼ cup (59 g) warm water, at 100°F

2 tablespoons (30 g) Einkorn Sourdough Starter (page 10), or a pinch of active dry yeast

1 cup (120 g) all-purpose einkorn flour

FOR THE BAGUETTE DOUGH

1½ cups (354 g) warm water, at 100°F

¼ teaspoon active dry yeast (omit for sourdough recipe)

5 cups (600 g) all-purpose einkorn flour, plus more for dusting

2 teaspoons fine sea salt

**1** MAKE THE PÂTE FERMENTÉE: In a medium bowl, mix together the water and starter or yeast until creamy. Add the flour and mix as much as possible. Knead the dough for 2 minutes until smooth. Return the dough to the bowl. Tightly seal with plastic wrap and let rest for 4 hours.

**2** MAKE THE BAGUETTE DOUGH: In a large bowl, add all of the *pâte fermentée* and the water. If baking with yeast, stir in additional yeast. Mix until the mixture is smooth and creamy. Add the flour and sprinkle the salt on top. Combine the ingredients with a stiff spatula as much as possible, then knead the dough in the bowl with your hands until it begins to hold together. Transfer the dough to a clean

work surface and knead it by hand for 1 minute until it has smoothed out. Place the dough back in the bowl, seal tightly with plastic wrap, and let rest for 1 hour.

**3** Lightly flour a work surface and transfer the dough to it. Dust the dough with flour and turn the dough (see page 15) once. Place it back in the bowl, cover, and let rest at room temperature for 3 to 5 hours.

**4** Lightly flour a work surface and transfer the dough to it. Divide the dough into 3 equal pieces. Fold and pat each piece into a rectangular shape that measures roughly 4 × 6 inches. Let the pieces rest, covered with a linen couche, for 10 minutes.

**5** Lightly dust your work surface with flour. Take the first piece of dough and fold the bottom long edge of the rectangle into the center, sealing the seam in the dough with the bottom of your thumb. Now fold the second edge into the center and seal tightly with the bottom of your thumb. Dust your hands with flour. With the seam side on the work surface, roll the dough with light pressure back and forth by moving your hands from the center outward to form a 12-inch-long cylinder. Press softly on the ends to form rounded edges, or press hard on the ends to create pointy edges.

**6** Line a rimless baking sheet with a linen couche and dust heavily with flour, allowing the linen to hang over the edges. Pick up the first baguette and place it on the sheet seam side down. Proceed in shaping the other pieces, placing them on the linen and leaving a fold of cloth on all sides of the loaves to support them tightly. Dust the tops of the loaves with flour and loosely cover them by folding over the ends of the linen. (Alternatively, shape the baguettes and place them on a baguette pan that has

been dusted with flour, then cover them with a linen couche.) Let proof at room temperature for 1 hour.

**7** Add 1½ inches of water to a baking dish and place in the bottom rack of your oven. Place a baking sheet on the center rack. Preheat the oven to 475°F.

**8** When the oven is heated, remove the hot baking sheet from the oven. With a quick motion, slide the 3 baguettes directly onto the baking sheet, and adjust them so they are equally spaced and lie straight on the sheet. Cut four 3-inch-long slashes in the top of each baguette at about a 20-degree angle. (If you are baking on the baguette pan, slash the loaves and place the pan in the oven on top of the baking sheet.)

**9** Bake for 25 minutes, rotating halfway through the cooking time. If the baguettes do not look very dark with a hint of deep browning, leave in the oven for 5 minutes more. Transfer to a wire rack to cool for 2 hours before slicing. These can be kept for 2 days, or freeze them for up to 1 month in a sealed plastic bag.

**THIS IS A FUN** project that will yield a large artisan loaf with a unique flavor and texture that I think you'll really love. Kefir is fermented milk that is 99 percent lactose free and contains three times more healthy probiotics than yogurt, including yeasts that will leaven bread. This bread will take three days to make, but that includes the time it takes to create a kefir sourdough starter. Of course, once you have the dough mixed, you can save some to use as a sourdough starter. This is a perfect way to create a quick starter without using commercial yeast, so if you do not have time to maintain a starter, you will always be able to re-create it with a bit of kefir.

MAKES ONE 8-INCH LOAF

# KEFIR SOURDOUGH BREAD

FOR THE KEFIR
SOURDOUGH STARTER

1 cup (120 g) all-purpose
einkorn flour

1 cup (240 g) kefir

FOR THE DOUGH

¾ cup (177 g) warm water, at
100°F

½ cup (120 g) kefir

6½ cups (780 g) all-purpose
einkorn flour, plus more for
dusting

1½ teaspoons fine sea salt

**1** MAKE THE STARTER: Combine the flour and kefir with a fork in a medium bowl until all of the flour has been absorbed. Transfer the mixture to a glass container and seal tightly. Let it rest for 48 hours at room temperature until the starter has risen up and become bubbly.

**2** MAKE THE DOUGH: In a large bowl, combine all of the kefir starter, the water, and the kefir. Add the flour, sprinkle salt on top of the flour, and mix together in the bowl with a stiff spatula until all of the flour is absorbed and you have a very sticky dough. Cover the bowl with plastic wrap and let proof at room temperature for 15 minutes.

**3** Heavily flour a work surface. Remove the dough from the bowl and turn it out onto the work area. Knead the dough a number of times until it is smooth and then form a rough ball. Place it back in the bowl and seal tightly with plastic wrap. Let it rest for 15 minutes.

**4** Turn the dough (see page 15) 3 times at 15-minute intervals. After the last turn, cover the bowl with plastic wrap and let proof for 12 to 15 hours at room temperature, or until the dough has risen by at least 30 percent. (If you would like to keep some kefir starter for future baking, detach 2 tablespoons (30 g) of the dough and follow the instructions on page 11 for feeding and finishing the starter.)

**5** Lightly flour a work surface. Remove the dough from the bowl and turn it out onto the work area. Knead the dough a number of times until smooth, and then form a round ball. Flip over the ball and stretch out the edges to form a 10-inch-long oval. Pull up each corner and the middle of each side, pressing them tightly into the center, to form a 6-inch round.

**6** Turn the dough over so the seam side is on the counter. Rotate the dough in a circular motion between your cupped hands until you have a tight round loaf. Dust the top of the loaf generously with flour.

**7** Line a colander with a linen couche that has been very heavily dusted with flour. Invert the loaf and place it in the colander seam side up. Dust with flour and then fold over the linen to cover the dough. Let proof for 90 minutes.

**8** Place a Dutch oven with the lid on in the oven. Preheat the oven to 450°F for 30 minutes.

**9** Remove the pot from the oven and remove the lid. Invert the loaf seam side down into the pan; shake the pan a bit if needed to center the loaf, but if it sticks to the side leave it as is. Cut four ¼-inch-deep slashes in the top of the loaf. Cover the pot and place it in the oven. Bake for 40 minutes.

**10** Remove the pot from the oven and take off the lid. If you like your loaf darker, return the uncovered pot to the oven for 5 minutes to brown the crust. Lift out the loaf and transfer it to a wire rack to cool for 2 hours before slicing. Wrap in a cotton or linen kitchen towel and store at room temperature for up to 3 days, or freeze in a sealed plastic bag for up to 1 month.

SANDWICH LOAVES MADE WITH einkorn flour can be difficult to get just right. This loaf is my version of soft American bread, made deeply golden and delicious with the added nutrients in einkorn. It is best to slice the bread after it has cooled completely. I like to bake 3 loaves at a time and freeze 2 of them. You may also fold raisins and cinnamon into the dough for a lovely breakfast bread, and this bread also turns out beautifully in the bread machine. MAKES 1 LOAF

# CLASSIC SANDWICH LOAF

1 batch Sourdough Levain (page 14) or Yeast Levain (page 14)

½ cup (122 g) whole milk, warmed to 100°F

¼ cup (60 g) warm water, at 100°F

2 tablespoons sugar

2¾ cups (330 g) all-purpose einkorn flour, plus more for dusting

1¼ teaspoons fine sea salt

2 tablespoons unsalted butter, melted and cooled, plus more for greasing the pan

1 In a medium bowl, combine the levain, milk, water, and sugar with a stiff spatula. In a large bowl, combine the flour and salt. Add the wet mixture to the flour and mix with a spatula until you have a shaggy dough. Work the butter into the dough until it is completely absorbed. Cover the bowl with a plate and let stand for 15 minutes.

2 Turn the dough (see page 15) 1 time. Cover the bowl tightly with plastic wrap and let rest for 3 to 5 hours. Generously butter an 8½ × 4½-inch loaf pan.

3 Lightly flour a work surface. Scrape the dough out of the bowl and transfer it to the work area. Spread out the dough by pulling gently on the edges to form an 8-inch-long oval. Fold the short edge of the oval to the center and press to close the seam tightly.

Repeat this step with the other side. Turn over the dough and rock on the work surface to seal the seam. Place the dough inside the pan, seam side down, but do not press down on the loaf. Cover with oiled plastic wrap. Let the dough proof at room temperature for 45 to 60 minutes, or until the top of the loaf rises ½ inch above the pan. Preheat the oven to 425°F.

4 Place the bread in the oven, then lower the temperature to 375°F. Bake the loaf for 40 minutes until golden brown. Place the pan on a wire rack to cool for 15 minutes, then turn out the loaf and let it cool completely for 2 hours before slicing. If you like a soft crust, place a clean towel over the loaf while it cools, so the steam is absorbed into the crust. Store in a sealed plastic bag for up to 3 days, or freeze for up to 1 month.

**WHOLE GRAIN EINKORN FLOUR** contains the entire outer layer of the whole grain, while all-purpose flour is a high-extraction milling with roughly 20 percent of the bran and germ removed. The added fiber of the bran will lend a sweet and nutty flavor to this 100 percent whole wheat sandwich loaf. The absorption of water takes some time with einkorn, so the dough will be wet and sticky, then stiffen just in time for shaping and baking. MAKES 1 LOAF

# WHOLE WHEAT SANDWICH LOAF

1 batch Sourdough Levain (page 14) or Yeast Levain (page 14)

½ cup (122 g) whole milk, warmed to 100°F

½ cup (118 g) warm water, at 100°F

1 tablespoon honey

4½ cups (432 g) whole grain einkorn flour, plus more for dusting

1¼ teaspoons fine sea salt

2 tablespoons melted and cooled unsalted butter, or extra-virgin olive oil

**1** In a medium bowl, combine the levain, milk, water, and honey with a stiff spatula. In a large bowl, combine the flour and salt. Add the wet mixture to the flour and mix with a spatula until the flour is absorbed. Work the butter into the dough until completely absorbed. Cover the bowl with a plate and let stand for 15 minutes.

**2** Turn the dough (see page 15) 1 time. Cover the bowl tightly with plastic wrap and let rest for 3 to 5 hours. Generously butter an 8½ × 4½-inch loaf pan.

**3** Lightly flour a work surface. Scrape the dough out of the bowl and transfer it to the work area. Spread out the dough by pulling gently on the edges to form an 8-inch-long oval, with the long side facing you. Pull and fold the top of the oval to the center, and

press with your fingertips to close the seam tightly. Repeat this step with the other side. Turn over the dough and rock on the work surface to seal the seam. Place the dough inside the pan seam side down and cover with oiled plastic wrap. Let the dough proof at room temperature for 1 hour until the top of the loaf rises above the rim of the pan. Preheat the oven to 425°F.

**4** Place the bread in the oven, then lower the temperature to 375°F. Bake the loaf for 35 to 40 minutes until golden brown on top. Place the pan on a wire rack to cool for 15 minutes, then turn out the loaf and let it cool completely for 2 hours before slicing. If you like a soft crust, place a clean towel over the loaf while it is cooling, so the steam is absorbed into the crust. Store in a sealed plastic bag for up to 3 days, or freeze for up to 1 month.

THIS IS A WONDERFULLY simple 100 percent whole grain artisan loaf that rises very nicely and has an enjoyable nutty flavor. A batard is an elongated, oval-shaped loaf and is great for evenly sized slices for sandwiches. To this basic whole grain recipe, you can add ingredients like pitted olives, herbs like rosemary, or nuts and seeds. You may also use the slices for making wholesome French toast. When my family is in the mood for whole grain bread, this is the recipe I turn to time after time. MAKES ONE 10-INCH LOAF

# WHOLE GRAIN BATARD

6 cups (576 g) whole grain einkorn flour, plus more for dusting

1½ teaspoons fine sea salt

1¼ cups (295 g) warm water, at 100°F

1 batch Sourdough Levain (page 14) or Yeast Levain (page 14)

**1** In a large bowl, mix together the flour and salt. In a medium bowl, add the water to the levain, mix to combine, and then pour it into the flour. Mix the ingredients with a stiff spatula until you have a sticky, wet dough. Cover the bowl and let stand for 15 minutes.

**2** Scrape around the bowl to loosen the dough. Lightly flour a work surface and transfer the dough to it. Turn the dough (see page 15) 3 times at 15-minute intervals. After the last turn, cover the bowl with plastic wrap and let proof at room temperature for 3 to 5 hours.

**3** Remove the dough from the bowl and turn it out onto the floured work area. Knead the dough until smooth, then shape it into a round ball. Flip over the ball and stretch out the edges to form a 10-inch-long oval. Pull up each corner and the middle of each side, and press them tightly into the center. Fold down the top and the bottom, pressing into the center to form a log. Roll back and forth on the work surface, tucking the edges underneath, to form a 9-inch-long cylinder

with all seams sealed. Heavily dust an 8½-inch unlined proofing basket with flour and invert the loaf into it. Cover with a linen couche or plastic wrap and let proof at room temperature for 1 hour.

**4** Add 1½ inches of water to a baking dish and place on a rack at the lowest position in the oven. Place a baking sheet on the middle rack. Preheat the oven to 425°F.

**5** Remove the baking sheet from the oven. Uncover the basket and forcefully flip the dough out of the basket and onto the baking sheet, tapping the basket if necessary to release the loaf. Cut one ¼-inch-deep slash down the center of the bread. Bake for 40 minutes until the crust is deeply browned, rotating the baking sheet after 20 minutes so the loaf browns evenly.

**6** Transfer the loaf to a wire rack to cool for 2 hours before slicing. Wrap the loaf in a clean cotton or linen towel for up to 3 days, or freeze in a plastic bag for up to 1 month.

**I LOVE THIS BREAD** because it has no added sugar, yet it satisfies a desire for something sweet and sustaining at breakfast. Nuts and raisins will give you energy, and so will the mix of all-purpose and whole grain einkorn flour, so it is a perfect way to start out the day. If you do want something sweeter, you could also make cinnamon raisin bread with this recipe—just omit the nuts and add 1 tablespoon cinnamon and ¼ cup sugar to the flour. MAKES ONE 8-INCH ROUND LOAF

# RAISIN AND WALNUT MICHE

1 cup (117 g) chopped walnuts

1 cup (145 g) raisins

3 cups (360 g) all-purpose einkorn flour, plus more for dusting

3 cups (288 g) whole grain einkorn flour

1½ teaspoons fine sea salt

1½ cups (354 g) warm water, at 100°F

1 batch Sourdough Levain (page 14) or Yeast Levain (page 14)

1 Place the walnuts and raisins in a small bowl and cover with 2 cups (472 g) of water. Soak for 1 hour. Place the walnuts and raisins in a fine mesh strainer until the water has drained off, at least 5 minutes. Gently squeeze out any excess soaking water.

2 In a medium bowl, combine the flours and salt. In a large bowl, combine the water and the levain. Add the flour mixture and mix with a spatula as much as you can. Add the walnuts and raisins and squeeze the dough between your hands until the flour has completely absorbed the water and the raisins and nuts are evenly distributed. Return the dough to the bowl, cover with a plate, and let stand for 15 minutes.

3 Lightly flour a work surface and transfer the dough to it. Turn the dough (see page 15) 1 time. Place back in the bowl, cover tightly with plastic wrap, and let rest at room temperature for 3 to 5 hours.

4 Lightly flour a work surface. Remove the dough from the bowl and turn it out onto the work area. Knead the dough a number of times until smooth, then form a round ball. Flip over the ball and stretch out the edges to form a 10-inch-long oval. Pull up each corner and the middle of each side, pressing them tightly into the center to form a 6-inch round. Turn the dough over so the seam side is on the counter. Rotate the dough in a circular motion between your cupped hands until you have a tight round shape. Dust the top of the loaf generously with flour.

5 Heavily dust a linen couche with flour and line a colander with it. Invert the loaf into the colander, dust with flour, and fold down the cloth to cover the dough. Proof at room temperature for 60 to 90 minutes.

**6** Place a Dutch oven with the lid on in the oven. Preheat the oven to 450°F for 30 minutes.

**7** Remove the pot from the oven and take off the lid. Invert the basket and drop the loaf in the pot. Slash two ¼-inch-deep strips across the top of the loaf lengthwise and three crosswise. Cover the pot and place in the oven. Bake for 40 minutes.

**8** Remove the pot from the oven and take off the lid. (If you like your loaf darker, return the uncovered pot to the oven for 5 minutes to brown the crust.) Remove the pot from the oven and lift out the loaf with oven mitts. Place on a wire rack to cool for 2 hours before slicing. Store in a sealed plastic bag for up to 3 days, or freeze for up to 1 month.

**THIS IS MY FAVORITE** type of bread to bake with einkorn flour. Since ciabatta bread requires a very wet and sticky dough, it is perfectly suited to einkorn bread baking. The more water you add to the dough, the bigger the bubble formation will be in the crumb. However, this can lead to some difficulty with shaping and proofing, especially the first time you make this recipe. That's why it's important to use an all-linen couche for this recipe in particular. There will be no need to introduce steam in the oven, because it will be naturally created as moisture evaporates from the dough.

MAKES ONE 13-INCH LOAF

# CIABATTA

1 batch Sourdough Levain (page 14) or Yeast Levain (page 14)

1¼ cups (295 g) warm water, at 100°F

4 cups (480 g) all-purpose einkorn flour, plus more for dusting

1½ teaspoons fine sea salt

1 In a large bowl, combine the levain and water with a stiff spatula. Add the flour and sprinkle the salt on top. Combine the ingredients with the spatula, forming a thick batter. Cover the bowl with a plate and let stand for 15 minutes.

2 Lightly flour a work surface. Use a dough scraper to transfer the dough onto the work area. Turn the dough (see page 15) 3 times every 15 minutes. With each turn, the dough should get slightly firmer but remain rather sticky. After the last turn, cover the bowl tightly with plastic wrap and let proof for 3 to 5 hours.

3 Place a linen couche on the table and dust heavily with flour. Heavily dust a clean work surface with flour. Turn out the dough on the work surface and dust the top of the dough with flour, using your fingers to gently

spread it over the dough. Fold the dough into thirds by folding the ends toward the center— you should end up with a nice tight rectangle. Stretch the rectangle out to about 12 inches long by tucking your hands under the dough and spreading the piece out. Place the dough in the center of the couche. Heavily dust the top of the loaf again. Fold the linen around the rectangle and let proof at room temperature for 60 to 90 minutes.

4 Place a baking sheet in the middle position of the oven and preheat the oven to 450°F.

5 Remove the baking sheet from the oven. Unfold the linen couche and gently flip the loaf onto the pan. Bake the bread for 35 minutes. Cool for 1 hour on a wire rack before slicing. Wrap in a cotton or linen kitchen towel and store at room temperature for up to 3 days, or freeze in a sealed plastic bag for up to 1 month.

WHETHER OR NOT YOU are interested in the health benefits of sprouted flour, you will surely agree that the extra flavor that the flour lends to this bread is fabulous. I have included the recipes for a loaf made with 25% sprouted flour, and another version with 100% sprouted flour. That slight malty flavor in the 25% loaf is very nice, whereas the 100% loaf is fairly dark in color and stronger flavored. I love both and feel that the extra step of sprouting the wheat berries is absolutely worth it. Instead of using a banneton basket after shaping the loaf, I use a colander lined with a linen couche, a technique that creates a less distinct pattern on the baked crust. MAKES ONE 10-INCH ROUND LOAF

# SPROUTED COUNTRY LOAF

FOR A 25% SPROUTED LOAF

1 cup (200 g) einkorn wheat berries or 2 cups (200 g) sprouted einkorn flour

2 cups (240 g) all-purpose einkorn flour

2 cups (192 g) whole grain einkorn flour, plus more for dusting

1½ teaspoons fine sea salt

1¼ cups (295 g) warm water, at 100°F

1 batch Sourdough Levain (page 14) or Yeast Levain (page 14)

FOR A 100% SPROUTED LOAF

3¼ cups (650 g) einkorn wheat berries, or 6½ cups (650 g) sprouted einkorn flour, plus more for dusting

1½ teaspoons fine sea salt

1½ cups (354 g) warm water, at 100°F

1 batch Sourdough Levain (page 14) or Yeast Levain (page 14)

**1** If starting with wheat berries, sprout, dehydrate, and grind the wheat berries to flour (see page 18).

**2** In a large bowl, combine the sprouted flour with the all-purpose and whole grain flours and salt. (If you are making the loaf with 100 percent sprouted flour, combine the sprouted flour and salt.) Add the water to the levain, mix to combine, and pour into the flour mixture. Mix the ingredients with a spatula as much as you can until you

have a sticky, wet dough. Cover the bowl with a plate and let stand at room temperature for 15 minutes.

**3** Lightly dust a clean work surface with flour. Scrape the dough out of the bowl, transfer it to the work area, and knead until smooth, using a dough scraper to help if the dough is sticky. Turn the dough (see page 15) 3 times at 15-minute intervals. After the last turn, cover the bowl tightly with plastic wrap and let proof for 3 to 5 hours.

**4** Lightly flour a work surface. Remove the dough from the bowl and transfer it to the work area. Knead the dough a number of times until smooth and then form a round ball. Flip over the ball and stretch out the edges to form a 10-inch-long oval. Pull up each corner and the middle of each side, pressing them tightly into the center to form a 6-inch round. Turn the dough over so the seam side is on the counter. Rotate the dough in a circular motion between your cupped hands until you have a tight round shape. Dust the top of the loaf generously with flour. Heavily dust a linen couche with flour and line a colander with it. Invert the loaf into the colander seam side up, dust with flour, and fold down the cloth to cover the dough. Proof at room temperature for 60 to 90 minutes.

**5** Place a Dutch oven with the lid on in the oven. Preheat the oven to 450°F for 30 minutes.

**6** Remove the pot from the oven and take off the lid. Flip the loaf out of the colander into the center of the pot seam side down. Shake a bit to center the loaf, but if it sticks to the side leave it as is. Cut four ¼-inch-deep slashes in the top of the loaf lengthwise and four more crosswise. Cover and place in the oven. Bake for 40 minutes.

**7** Remove the pot from the oven and take off the lid. (If you like your loaf darker, return the uncovered pot to the oven for 5 minutes to brown the crust.) Lift out the loaf and transfer it to a wire rack to cool for 2 hours before slicing. Wrap in a cotton or linen kitchen towel and store at room temperature for up to 3 days, or freeze in a sealed plastic bag for up to 1 month.

**IF CIABATTA IS MY** favorite bread to bake with einkorn, I would say this focaccia is the runner-up. Again, because focaccia dough is traditionally wet and sticky, it's perfect for einkorn. Many recipes call for a lot of oil in the dough, but authentic focaccia actually has a fairly low fat content in the dough and a touch of white wine. Instead of sprinkling sea salt on top of the dough, which can continue to cook the bread after baking and create white spots, I like to brush the bread with an oil and salt emulsion to create that salty and oily crust everyone loves. You can choose one or more of the optional toppings; I like to make 4 different sections to please everyone in the family.

MAKES ONE 13 × 18-INCH FOCACCIA

# FOCACCIA GENOVESE

FOR THE DOUGH

1 batch Sourdough Levain (page 14) or Yeast Levain (page 14)

1 cup plus 1 tablespoon (250 g) warm water, at 100°F

¼ cup (50 g) extra-virgin olive oil, plus more for greasing the baking sheet

1 tablespoon dry white wine

4 cups (480 g) all-purpose einkorn flour, plus more for dusting

2 teaspoons fine sea salt

FOR THE OPTIONAL TOPPINGS (PER BATCH)

1½ (160 g) cups shredded cheese, such as provolone or Fontina

1 large onion, thinly sliced

3 tablespoons snipped fresh rosemary leaves

2 cups halved cherry tomatoes

1 **MAKE THE DOUGH:** In a large bowl, combine the levain, the 1 cup (236 g) water, 2 tablespoons of the oil, and the wine. Add the flour on top, and then sprinkle with 1 teaspoon of the salt. Mix with a stiff spatula until all of the flour is absorbed. Cover the bowl with a plate and let rest at room temperature for 15 minutes.

2 Lightly flour a work surface. Remove the dough from the bowl, scraping the sides of the bowl with your fingers or a dough scraper, and turn it out onto the work area. Turn the dough (see page 15) 3 times at 15-minute intervals. The very sticky dough

will not hold its shape and will sag at first, but after a few turns you will notice it has more structure. Cover the bowl and let proof at room temperature for 3 hours.

3 In a small bowl, mix together the remaining 2 tablespoons oil, 1 tablespoon water, and 1 teaspoon salt with a fork until the salt has melted. Grease a 13 × 18-inch rimmed baking sheet.

4 Lift the dough from the bowl and place in the center of the prepared pan. Dip your hands in the oil and salt emulsion. Stretch and press the dough evenly to cover the entire pan. Line

up your hands next to each other and use your fingers to make even rows of deep indentations (but not holes) in the dough. Pour the remaining emulsion evenly over the focaccia, tilting the pan to fill up most of the indentations.

5 Add the additional toppings of your choice. Cover with plastic wrap and let proof for 2 hours.

6 Preheat the oven to 425°F. Bake the focaccia for 20 to 22 minutes until the edges are golden brown and crispy and the center is still fairly soft and lightly golden. Cool in the pan for 30 minutes before slicing. Store at room temperature wrapped in parchment paper for up to 2 days, or freeze in a sealed plastic bag for up to 1 month. To serve, heat in a preheated oven to 375°F for 10 minutes.

**WITH LOTS OF TOMATOES** simmered in garlic and rosemary, these mini-focaccia make a fun and healthy sandwich or snack. The whole grain flour adds a wholesome flavor and soft texture to the bread. When you mix the dough, it will have the texture of thick muffin batter at first, but during proofing the flour will absorb the water, so you will be able to shape the rounds before baking. MAKES 12 MINI-FOCACCIA

# TOMATO AND ROSEMARY WHOLE GRAIN FOCACCIA ROUNDS

FOR THE TOMATO BASE

6 tablespoons (80 g) extra-virgin olive oil

8 ounces (1½ cups) cherry tomatoes, quartered

1 garlic clove, minced

¼ teaspoon fine sea salt

⅛ teaspoon dried oregano

½ cup (75 g) pitted and sliced green olives (optional)

Leaves from two 3-inch sprigs of fresh rosemary, snipped with kitchen shears

FOR THE FOCACCIA DOUGH

1 batch Sourdough Levain (page 14) or Yeast Levain (page 14)

⅔ cup (157 g) warm water, at 100°F

5 cups (480 g) whole grain einkorn flour, plus more for dusting

1½ teaspoons fine sea salt

Extra-virgin olive oil, for greasing the pan and forming the rounds

**1 MAKE THE TOMATO BASE:** Heat 2 tablespoons of the oil in a medium skillet. Add the tomatoes, garlic, salt, and oregano. Cook on medium heat for 5 minutes. Transfer to a small bowl and let cool for 10 minutes. Mix in the remaining ¼ cup oil, the olives, and the rosemary.

**2 MAKE THE DOUGH:** In a large bowl, mix the levain and water until the levain has dissolved. Add the flour and sprinkle the salt over the flour. Mix together with a spatula as much as you can. Add the tomato-olive base and squeeze the dough in your hands until the olives and tomatoes are evenly distributed and the dough has absorbed the oil. Cover the bowl with plastic wrap tightly and let rest for 3 to 5 hours.

**3** Flour a work surface and scrape the dough onto it. Divide the dough into 12 equal pieces. Generously oil a rimmed baking sheet.

**4** In a small bowl, mix together 1 tablespoon of water and 1 tablespoon of oil. Dip your hands in the mixture. Roll each piece of dough in your hands to form a ball. Place each ball on the baking sheet and press into a 3½-inch round, using the tips of your fingers to make indentations. Cover with lightly oiled plastic wrap and let rest for 60 to 90 minutes.

**5** Preheat the oven to 425°F. Bake the focaccia for 18 to 20 minutes until slightly brown on the edges. Let cool for 15 minutes before serving. Store the focaccia in a plastic bag for up to 3 days, or freeze for up to 1 month.

**IT IS INTERESTING HOW** an hour's drive can change people, food, accents, and architecture so much in Italy. People in Lucca like their bread with salt, contrary to the stereotype that all Tuscan bread is saltless, while Florentines eat this type of salt-free bread. It's a great accompaniment to rich stews and can also be used to make bruschetta. Without the salt, the loaf will remain lighter in color when baked, so don't wait for it to brown. MAKES ONE 10-INCH LOAF

# PANE TOSCANO

FOR THE STARTER DOUGH

½ cup (118 g) warm water, at 100°F

2 tablespoons (30 g) refreshed Einkorn Sourdough Starter (page 13), or ⅛ teaspoon active dry yeast

2 cups (240 g) all-purpose einkorn flour, plus more for dusting

FOR THE FINAL DOUGH

1 cup (236 g) warm water, at 100°F

¼ teaspoon active dry yeast (omit for sourdough)

3⅓ cups (400 g) all-purpose einkorn flour

**1** MAKE THE STARTER DOUGH: In a large bowl, combine the water and starter or yeast and mix until dissolved. Add the flour and knead in the bowl until the dough comes together. Lightly flour a work surface. Transfer the dough to the work area and knead for 1 minute until smooth. Return the dough to the bowl, cover tightly with plastic wrap, and proof at room temperature for 8 to 10 hours.

**2** MAKE THE FINAL DOUGH: Add the water to the starter dough. If you are making the bread with yeast, stir in the yeast. For sourdough bread, you will not need additional starter. Mix with a stiff spatula until the mixture is smooth and creamy. Add the flour and continue to mix as much as you can. Knead with your hands in the bowl until the dough comes together. Lightly flour a work surface and transfer the dough to it. Knead by hand for 1 to 2 minutes until

the dough gets smoother and sticky. Cover the bowl with plastic wrap and let rest for 1 hour.

**3** Lightly flour a work surface and transfer the dough to it. Knead the dough into a ball, and then roll back and forth on the work surface until it forms a rough cylindrical shape that is about 6 inches long. Dust the work surface again, place the dough on top, and dust the top of the dough again. Cover the dough with a linen couche. Let rest for 10 minutes.

**4** Fold the bottom long edge of the dough into the center, pressing the seam to seal. Fold the opposite edge all the way to the other side and seal tightly with the bottom. Dust your hands with flour. Place the seam side on the bottom. Roll the dough back and forth into a 10-inch-long cylinder that is 1½ inches in height. Generously dust the linen couche with flour and place the loaf seam side down in the

center. Generously dust the top of the loaf, then wrap the linen tightly around the dough so it holds its shape. Let proof for 1 hour.

**5** Place a baking sheet in the oven. Preheat to 425°F.

**6** Open the linen and roll the loaf onto the baking sheet. Bake for 30 minutes. Transfer to a wire rack and let cool for 2 hours before slicing. Wrap in a cotton or linen kitchen towel and store at room temperature for up to 3 days, or freeze in a sealed plastic bag for up to 1 month.

**THIS IS THE FIRST** bread roll recipe I ever developed, and it has been in my family for many years. The addition of sugar and a bit of olive oil and the combination of whole grain and all-purpose flours create a soft and chewy roll that is perfect for sandwiches. The proofing times are quicker for these rolls than for larger loaves, so this is a great option when you are short on time. Forming the traditional Kaiser roll shape takes a bit of practice, but do not worry about getting it perfect because the floral shape will fill out nicely when the rolls spring up in the oven.

MAKES 12 ROLLS

# SEMI-WHOLE GRAIN KAISER ROLLS

1 batch Sourdough Levain (page 14) or Yeast Levain (page 14)

1⅓ cups (315 g) warm water, at 100°F

3 tablespoons extra-virgin olive oil

2 tablespoons sugar

4 cups (384 g) whole grain einkorn flour, plus more for dusting

3½ cups (420 g) all-purpose einkorn flour

1½ teaspoons fine sea salt

1  In a medium bowl, mix together the levain, water, oil, and sugar until creamy. In a large bowl, combine the flours and salt. Add the liquid mixture to the flour mixture and mix with a spatula as much as you can. Knead the dough in the bowl until it holds together. Turn out on a clean work surface and knead by hand briefly until the dough gets sticky. Return the dough to the bowl, cover tightly with plastic wrap, and let proof at room temperature for 2 to 4 hours. Line a rimmed baking sheet with parchment paper.

2  Divide the dough into quarters. Lightly flour a work surface. Transfer each piece to the work area and divide the pieces into thirds.

Roll each third of dough into a 12-inch-long rope. Form a circle with the dough, then tie a snug knot. Fold one end under the circle and then press it into the center, and then fold the other end over and into the center on the other side, pressing to seal. Place the rolls on the baking sheet 2 inches apart. Cover with oiled plastic wrap and let proof for 60 minutes. Preheat the oven to 425°F.

3  Bake the rolls for 20 minutes until the rolls are deeply golden brown on the bottom. Transfer the rolls to a wire rack to cool completely. (If you would like a softer crust, drape a clean and dry kitchen towel on top of the bread while it cools.) Store in a sealed plastic bag for up to 3 days, or freeze for up to 1 month.

**THE PRESENTATION OF THIS** bread is lovely, with a simple three-stranded braid, and adding eggs creates a soft, delicate flavor and texture. (This recipe can also be divided into 8 pieces and shaped into small braided or round rolls; if you decide to do that, just reduce the baking time to 25 minutes.) MAKES ONE 12-INCH LOAF

# BRAIDED EGG BREAD

1 batch Sourdough Levain (page 14) or Yeast Levain (page 14)

3 large eggs, 1 separated

3 tablespoons unsalted butter, melted and cooled, or vegetable oil

3 tablespoons sugar

3 cups (360 g) all-purpose einkorn flour, plus more for dusting

1¼ teaspoons fine sea salt

**1** In a medium bowl, mix together the levain, 2 eggs, the separated egg yolk, butter or oil, and sugar until the mixture is creamy.

**2** In a large bowl, combine the flour and salt. Add the egg mixture to the flour and mix the dough with a stiff spatula as much as you can. Lightly flour a work surface and transfer the dough to it.

**3** Knead by hand for 2 minutes until the dough is very smooth and a bit sticky. Return the dough to the bowl, cover with a plate, and let rest for 15 minutes. Turn the dough (see page 15) one time. Cover the bowl tightly with plastic wrap and let proof at room temperature for 3 to 6 hours.

**4** Transfer the dough to a clean work surface and knead it gently a few times until smooth. Divide the dough into 3 equal pieces. Shape each piece into a 6-inch-long

rope. Cover with plastic wrap and let rest for 15 minutes.

**5** Line a rimmed baking sheet with parchment paper. Roll out each cylinder of dough to a firm 12-inch-long strand. Place 2 strands on the sheet in the form of an upside-down V, and press the top ends together. Add the third strand as a straight line down the middle, pressing the strand on top of where the others are joined. Cross the left strand over to lie between the middle strand and the right strand. Cross the right strand over to lie between the new middle strand and the outer left strand. Continue like this until you arrive at the end of the dough. To seal the bottom seam, press the last piece on top of the other two. Cover the braid with lightly oiled plastic wrap, tucking it tightly around to prevent a skin from forming, and let proof at room temperature for 90 minutes.

6 Preheat the oven to 350°F. Beat together the reserved egg white and 1 tablespoon of water and brush the entire surface with the egg wash. Bake the bread for 30 to 35 minutes until lightly golden brown on top.

7 Transfer the bread to a wire rack, cover with a clean kitchen towel, and cool for 1 hour before slicing. Store in a sealed plastic bag for up to 3 days, or freeze for up to 1 month.

**THE ADDITION OF YOGURT** and a long fermentation time give this corn bread a slightly tangy flavor and a light, fluffy texture. Be sure to use finely ground cornmeal for the best results. You may also convert this recipe from a lightly sweetened corn bread to a savory one by adding 1½ cups shredded Cheddar cheese and 4 thinly sliced jalapeño peppers before folding in the butter.

MAKES ONE 10-INCH TUBE OR 9-INCH ROUND

# EINKORN CORN BREAD

1 batch Sourdough Levain (page 14) or Yeast Levain (page 14)

1 cup (245 g) plain yogurt

½ cup (118 g) warm water, at 100°F

2 large eggs

⅓ cup (67 g) sugar

1½ teaspoons fine sea salt

2 cups (240 g) all-purpose einkorn flour

1½ cups (200 g) finely ground yellow cornmeal

6 tablespoons (85 g) unsalted butter, melted and cooled, plus more for greasing the pan

**1** In a large bowl, combine the levain, yogurt, water, eggs, sugar, and salt. Add the flour and cornmeal and combine with a stiff spatula until all of the flour is absorbed. Fold in the butter until you have a thick batter. Cover the bowl tightly with plastic wrap and let rest for 3 to 5 hours until the dough has expanded and is bubbly under the surface.

**2** Generously butter a 10-inch tube pan or a 9-inch springform pan. Drop the dough into the pan evenly in dollops with a large spoon. Wet a spatula with cold water and use it to evenly spread out the surface of the dough. Cover with plastic wrap and let proof for 90 minutes.

**3** Preheat the oven to 425°F.

**4** Bake the bread for 45 minutes until it is deeply golden. Place the pan on a wire rack to cool for 15 minutes, then invert the pan onto a serving platter (if using a tube pan), or remove the bottom of the springform pan and transfer the bread to a platter. Serve warm. If not eating right away, you can store the corn bread in a sealed plastic bag for up to 3 days, or freeze for up to 1 month.

**BAGELS MADE WITH EINKORN** flour are absolutely delicious. If you have never made homemade bagels, you might not realize how many phases the dough goes through. It is mixed, proofed, and shaped and then boiled in water and baking soda before its final baking. When the bagels hit the boiling water, the starches in the flour gelatinize and form a thick crust, while the baking soda helps them brown up in the oven. Once the crust is set, the dough won't rise as much as a regular loaf of bread, creating that dense chewiness inside that bagel lovers crave.

MAKES 10 BAGELS

# BAGELS

1 batch Sourdough Levain (page 14) or Yeast Levain (page 14)

¾ cup (177 g) warm water, at 100°F

2 teaspoons pure maple syrup

4½ cups (540 g) all-purpose einkorn flour

2 teaspoons fine sea salt

Extra-virgin olive oil, for brushing the baking sheet

1 teaspoon baking soda

Sesame seeds, poppy seeds, caraway seeds, crushed red pepper flakes, dry herbs, garlic, and/or onion for topping (optional)

**1** In a medium bowl, mix together the levain, water, and maple syrup until creamy. In a large bowl, combine the flour and salt. Add the liquid mixture to the flour and mix with a stiff spatula as much as you can. Squeeze the dough in your hands until the dough holds together. Turn out on a clean work surface and knead by hand briefly until the dough just gets sticky. Return to the bowl and cover tightly with plastic wrap. Let proof for 2 to 3 hours.

**2** Transfer the dough to a clean work surface. Divide the dough into 10 equal pieces and create tight rounds by rolling each piece with pressure in a circular motion to form a ball. To form the bagels, roll each ball into

a tight 6-inch rope. Loop the dough to form a circle. Press one end over the other to seal. Brush a baking sheet with olive oil. Place the shaped bagels on the sheet, then cover with plastic wrap lightly brushed with oil and let rest for 45 minutes. Place a baking sheet in the oven and preheat to 500°F.

**3** Bring 2 quarts of water to a rolling boil. Lower the heat so the water is barely boiling, then add the baking soda. It will foam up and subside, then increase the heat to maintain a boil. Test a bagel by dropping it in the boiling water; it should float up to the surface pretty quickly. If not, place back on the tray and proof the bagels for 30 minutes.

**4** Cook 3 bagels at a time for 45 seconds until the bagels expand and turn dark yellow, flipping after 20 seconds. Lift up the bagels with a slotted spoon and transfer to a cooling rack. If you wish to add seeds or spices to the bagels, let the bagels rest for 2 minutes, then pick up each bagel with your hands and press the topside into the toppings.

**5** Remove the hot baking sheet from the oven and line it with a new piece of parchment paper. Position the bagels 1 inch apart on the sheet.

**6** Bake the bagels for 13 minutes until golden brown. Transfer the bagels to a wire rack to cool for 15 minutes before serving. Store in a sealed plastic bag for up to 3 days, or freeze for up to 1 month.

THESE ROLLS HAVE BEEN on my family's Thanksgiving table for many years. Soft and delicate, they are tasty as a dinner roll, served warm with butter, and great for leftover turkey sandwiches. I also love to toast them at breakfast and eat them with a spoonful of honey. For soft styles of einkorn bread like this, you must keep the dough moist, so when you form the rolls the dough might seem overly sticky. Dust the rolls and your hands minimally with flour during shaping, but make sure you are using pressure when rolling them tight, or they might crack during baking. Choose sweet potatoes with the deepest orange flesh for beautifully colored rolls. MAKES 16 ROLLS

# SWEET POTATO ROLLS

1½ pounds (500 g) Garnet sweet potatoes (2 medium), mashed (about 2 cups)

¼ cup (60 g) whole milk

4 tablespoons (56 g) unsalted butter, plus more for greasing the baking sheets

1 batch Sourdough Levain (page 14) or Yeast Levain (page 14)

1 large egg

½ cup (100 g) sugar

1 teaspoon apple cider vinegar

2 teaspoons fine sea salt

6¼ cups (750 g) all-purpose einkorn flour, plus more for dusting

1 Preheat the oven to 375°F. Scrub the sweet potatoes and slice a small piece off one end of each potato. Place in a large baking dish and bake for 60 to 75 minutes, or until the potatoes are very soft. Allow to cool until cool enough to handle, about 10 minutes, then peel and mash well in a large bowl.

2 Add the milk and butter to the bowl.

3 Stir the levain, egg, sugar, vinegar, and salt into the sweet potatoes with a spatula. Add the flour and mix until combined. Knead the dough in the bowl until the dough becomes smooth and sticky. Cover the bowl with plastic wrap and let proof for 3 to 5 hours.

4 Butter 2 baking sheets or line them with parchment paper. Divide the dough into 16 equal pieces. Dust your hands and a work surface lightly with flour. Roll each piece of dough into a tight ball. Divide the rolls between the baking sheets, placing each 2 inches apart. Cover with buttered plastic wrap and let proof for 90 minutes. Preheat the oven to 400°F.

5 Bake the rolls, one sheet at a time, for 20 to 23 minutes until they start to brown slightly on top. (Watch closely, as they burn easily on the bottom.) Transfer the rolls to a wire rack and let cool for 30 minutes. Serve warm or at room temperature. Store any leftover rolls in a sealed plastic bag for up to 3 days, or freeze for up to 1 month.

**THIS BASIC SOFT BUN** recipe can be shaped either round for hamburgers and sandwiches (or for great dinner rolls), or rolled out long for hot dogs. As with Sweet Potato Rolls (page 63), wetter dough will bake up to be soft and moist, so try to use just enough flour to be able to work the dough and have patience with the stickiness. You may substitute any sweetener for the sugar, and also make the recipe dairy-free by using all water in the dough. MAKES 12 HAMBURGER OR HOT DOG BUNS

# HAMBURGER AND HOT DOG BUNS

1 batch Sourdough Levain (page 14) or Yeast Levain (page 14)

⅓ cup (80 g) warm water, at 100°F

⅓ cup (80 g) warm whole milk, at 100°F

3 large eggs

2 tablespoons unsalted butter, melted and cooled

2 tablespoons extra-virgin olive oil, plus more for greasing the pans and plastic wrap

¼ cup (50 g) sugar

5 cups (600 g) all-purpose einkorn flour, plus more for dusting

2 teaspoons fine sea salt

Sesame seeds, for topping hamburger buns (optional)

1 large egg white

**1** In a medium bowl, combine the levain, water, milk, eggs, butter, oil, and sugar; beat until the yolks and whites have been combined. In a large bowl, mix together the flour and salt. Add the wet mixture to the flour mixture and mix with a spatula as much as you can. Knead the dough in the bowl with your hands until you have a rough, sticky dough. Cover the bowl with a plate and let rest for 15 minutes.

**2** Turn the dough 2 times (see page 15) at 15-minute intervals. After the last turn, cover the bowl tightly with plastic wrap and let proof for 3 to 5 hours.

**3** Grease 2 baking sheets. Lightly flour a work surface and transfer the dough to it.

**4** MAKE HAMBURGER BUNS: Use a dough scraper or knife to divide the dough into 12 pieces. Dust your hands with flour, and shape each piece into a round by rolling and pressing the dough in a tight circle. Place them 2 inches apart on the baking sheets. Pat the buns down to flatten to about 1 inch high. Cover with oiled plastic wrap and let proof for 90 minutes.

**5** **MAKE HOT DOG BUNS:** Use a dough scraper or knife to divide the dough into 12 pieces. Roll each piece of dough into a tight circle, then press to elongate into a 6-inch cylinder shape. Place them in a hot dog pan or on the baking sheets. Cover with oiled plastic wrap and let proof for 90 minutes. Preheat the oven to 375°F.

**6** For a deeper color, mix the egg white with 1 teaspoon of water and brush the tops of the rolls. (If you would like to add sesame seeds, sprinkle them on top now.) Bake the rolls 1 sheet at a time for 20 to 22 minutes until they start to brown slightly on top.

**7** Lift the rolls up with a metal spatula and let cool on a wire rack for 30 minutes. Serve warm or at room temperature. The rolls can be stored in a sealed plastic bag for up to 3 days, or freeze for up to 1 month.

**IF YOU'VE YET TO** experience the magic of watching homemade pita breads puff up in the oven, you are going to love this recipe. That's what makes this a great baking experience for little ones, who will keep their eyes on the oven for you. It's important not to let the einkorn pitas brown, as they will lose their softness. If you would like to make sourdough pita, simply substitute ¼ cup (60 g) of refreshed Einkorn Sourdough Starter (page 13) for the yeast and lengthen the first proofing time to 6 to 8 hours. MAKES TEN 6-INCH PITAS

# PITA BREAD

1 cup (236 g) warm water, at 100°F

½ teaspoon active dry yeast

4 cups (480 g) all-purpose einkorn flour, or 4¾ cups (456 g) whole grain einkorn flour, plus more for dusting

1½ teaspoons fine sea salt

**1** In a small bowl, combine the water and yeast until the yeast is dissolved. In a large bowl, mix together the flour and salt. Add the yeast mixture to the flour and mix together with a spatula as much as you can. Knead the dough with your hands until it holds together. Transfer to a clean work surface and knead for 1 minute until the dough is smooth and a bit sticky. Place the dough back in the bowl, cover tightly with plastic wrap, and let proof for 1 hour.

**2** Lightly flour a work surface and transfer the dough to it. Divide the dough into 10 equal pieces. (Cover the pieces of dough with plastic wrap until you're ready to shape them.) Roll out each piece of dough to a 6-inch round. Heavily dust a linen couche

or a sheet of parchment paper with flour and place the dough rounds on it. Rub the top of the pita with more flour and cover with a linen couche. Let rest for 45 minutes.

**3** Place a baking sheet in the oven. Preheat the oven to 450°F.

**4** Remove the baking sheet from the oven, and place 2 to 3 pitas on the sheet. Bake for 4 to 5 minutes until they have puffed up completely but not browned. (Not all pitas may puff up, but remove them before they brown.) Wrap the cooked pitas in a clean kitchen towel while you continue to bake the rest. Serve warm. The pitas can be stored in a sealed plastic bag for up to 3 days or frozen for up to 1 month.

RYE AND EINKORN ARE kindred spirits. Both grew many thousands of years ago in the Fertile Crescent, but unlike einkorn, rye made a comeback during the Middle Ages, when it was widely cultivated in central and eastern Europe. I love highlighting their hearty flavors with caraway seeds, especially for a grilled cheese sandwich with homemade red cabbage sauerkraut.

MAKES ONE 12-INCH LOAF

# DELI-STYLE EINKORN RYE BREAD

1 batch Sourdough Levain (page 14) or Yeast Levain (page 14)

1 cup (236 g) warm water, at 100°F

1 tablespoon honey

2 tablespoons extra-virgin olive oil or vegetable oil

2¼ cups (270 g) all-purpose einkorn flour, plus more for dusting

2 cups (240 g) whole grain rye flour

1 cup (96 g) whole grain einkorn flour

2 tablespoons whole caraway seeds

1¾ teaspoons fine sea salt

**1** In a medium bowl, combine the levain, water, honey, and oil. In a large bowl, mix together the flours, caraway seeds, and salt. Add the liquid mixture to the flour and mix with a spatula as much as possible. Knead the dough with your hands until it just holds together. Cover the bowl with a plate and let rest for 15 minutes. Turn the dough (see page 15) once. Return the dough to the bowl, cover, and let proof at room temperature for 2 to 4 hours.

**2** Lightly flour a work surface and scrape the dough out onto it. Spread out the dough by pulling gently on the edges to form an 8-inch-long oval. Pull and fold one long side of the oval to the center. Press with your fingertips to close the seam tightly; repeat with the other side. Turn over the dough and

rock on the work surface to seal the seam and create a 10-inch-long cylinder. Place the loaf directly on an oiled baking sheet and make five ¼-inch-deep slashes across the bread. Cover the dough with oiled plastic wrap and let proof for 60 minutes.

**3** Add 1½ inches of water to a baking dish and place on a rack at the lowest position in the oven. Preheat the oven to 425°F.

**4** Bake for 35 minutes, or until evenly browned. Transfer the loaf to a cooling rack and allow to cool for 2 hours before slicing. If you like a soft crust, drape a clean towel over the loaf while it cools. Wrap in a cotton or linen towel and store at room temperature for up to 3 days, or freeze in a sealed plastic bag for up to 1 month.

TORTILLAS ARE VERY EASY to make and nice to have available for sandwich wraps. Unfortunately, they stay fresh for only a few days. Luckily, it's easy to turn them into tortilla chips: Cut the tortillas into wedges, brush with olive oil, and season with your favorite spices, then bake in a 350°F oven for 22 minutes, rotating halfway through, until they are nice and crispy. MAKES TWELVE 8-INCH TORTILLAS

# FLOUR TORTILLAS

4 cups (480 g) all-purpose einkorn flour, plus more for dusting

1½ teaspoons fine sea salt

½ teaspoon baking powder

1 cup (236 g) warm water, at 100°F

3 tablespoons leaf lard, at room temperature, or extra-virgin olive oil

**1** In a large bowl, combine the flour, salt, and baking powder. Combine the water and lard in a small bowl. Add the wet mixture to the flour. Mix the dough with a spatula as much as you can, then knead the dough in the bowl until it forms a ball. Cover with a plate and let rest for 15 minutes.

**2** Lightly flour a work surface and transfer the dough to it. Knead the dough for 1 minute until smooth. Heat a cast-iron skillet or griddle on medium heat for 10 minutes.

**3** Divide the dough into 12 equal pieces and form into balls. Lightly dust a ball of dough with flour. Use a rolling pin to roll out the dough to 8 inches in diameter, rubbing the round lightly with flour as needed.

**4** Place a tortilla on the griddle. The temperature is correct when you hear the dough sizzle, but the tortilla does not burn. Cook for 45 seconds to 1 minute on each side until the dough is light in color and the surface has browned in spots. Wrap the tortilla in a clean kitchen towel to keep it warm and soft while you roll out and cook the rest of the tortillas. Serve warm. The tortillas can be stored in a sealed plastic bag for up to 2 days at room temperature or frozen for up to 1 month.

THIS STYLE OF BREAD STICKS was invented in Torino in the late seventeenth century for the future king of Savoy, who had problems digesting bread. The baker emulated the shape of the typical regional bread, which was long like a baguette, but then stretched the dough to very thin strips that baked up crispy all the way through, because it was believed only the white crumb was hard to digest. The irregularly shaped thin ropes of dough are what make these homemade bread sticks so distinctive. To make the authentic shape, you will need to slice thin strips of dough and roll them out as slender as you can without tearing. MAKES ABOUT 3 DOZEN BREAD STICKS

# THIN GRISSINI

1 batch Sourdough Levain (page 14) or Yeast Levain (page 14)

⅓ cup (80g) warm water, at 100°F

3 tablespoons extra-virgin olive oil, plus more for greasing the baking sheets

3 cups (360 g) all-purpose einkorn flour, plus more for dusting

1¼ teaspoons fine sea salt

1 In a medium bowl, mix together the levain, water, and oil until creamy. In a large bowl, combine the flour and salt. Add the wet mixture to the flour and mix with a spatula as much as you can. Transfer the dough to a clean work surface and knead by hand for 1 minute until the dough is smooth. Return the dough to the bowl and cover tightly with plastic wrap. Let proof for 3 hours.

2 Lightly flour a work surface and transfer the dough to it. Knead the dough a few times to smooth it out, then shape into a 6 × 8-inch rectangle. Brush 2 baking sheets with oil.

3 With a dough scraper or knife, cut off a strip of dough that is ⅜ inch wide from the short side of the rectangle. Roll out into a long, thin rope by moving your hands from

the center out to the ends with light pressure. The grissini should be as long as the width of the baking sheet and have a diameter of roughly ¼ inch; thicker sections may not crisp while baking.

4 Place each piece on the baking sheet, spaced about ¼ inch apart. When the first sheet is full, cover with oiled plastic wrap and repeat with the second sheet. Let proof for 30 minutes. Preheat the oven to 400°F.

5 Bake the grissini for 22 minutes until they are pale golden and crispy, rotating the position of the sheets halfway through the cooking time. The grissini will crisp up more after cooling. Transfer to a cooling rack to cool completely. The grissini can be stored in an airtight container at room temperature for up to 5 days.

**I CREATED THIS RECIPE** one day when my daughter was home sick from elementary school and looking for something to snack on. She was thoroughly impressed by their appearance and I was happy to discover how easy it was to make great-tasting homemade crackers. I learned to work in small batches because rolling out smaller pieces of einkorn dough helps you to get it very thin so the crackers bake up light and crispy. If you want to add dry herbs, sprinkle 1/8 teaspoon on each batch and gently rub into the surface of the dough before baking. MAKES ABOUT 10 DOZEN CRACKERS

# SEA SALT CRACKERS

2½ cups (300 g) all-purpose einkorn flour

¼ teaspoon baking powder

¼ teaspoon fine sea salt

½ cup (118 g) water, at 100°F

¼ cup (50 g) extra-virgin olive oil

1 teaspoon flaky or coarse sea salt, for dusting

**1** Add 1½ inches of water to a baking dish and place on the bottom rack of your oven. Place a rimmed baking sheet on the center rack. Preheat the oven to 400°F.

**2** In a large bowl, combine the flour, baking powder, and sea salt. In a small bowl, combine the water and the oil and beat with a fork until emulsified. Add to the flour mixture and mix with a spatula as much as you can. Knead the dough in the bowl with your hands until the dough comes together. Rub the dough against the sides of the bowl to collect any remaining flour, then turn it out onto your work surface and knead by hand about 20 times until smooth. Divide the dough into quarters, and cover it with plastic wrap to keep moist.

**3** Cut a piece of parchment paper to fit your baking sheet. Use a rolling pin to roll out the first piece of dough as thin as possible on the paper, lifting frequently, until you have a

10 × 10-inch square. (Take your time in rolling the dough as thin as you possibly can.) With a fluted pastry wheel, trim the edges to make a perfect square, then cut the rectangle into 2-inch rows vertically and horizontally to form square crackers. Return the scraps of dough to the bowl. Dust the surface of the dough with ¼ teaspoon flaky salt.

**4** Carefully remove the baking sheet from the oven and slide the sheet of parchment with the crackers onto the pan. Bake for 9 to 10 minutes until the crackers have just turned golden. Pick up the paper and slide the crackers into a large serving bowl to cool.

**5** Return the baking sheet to the oven to warm up again, then proceed with rolling, seasoning, and baking the remaining portions of dough in the same manner. The crackers can be stored at room temperature in an airtight container for up to 3 days.

**I LIVE IN EMILIA-ROMAGNA,** the region of Italy that is famous for Parmigiano-Reggiano cheese, which my daughter Livia affectionately nicknamed "Parmy" when she was little. If Parmigiano is hard to find where you live or too pricey, you can substitute your choice of finely grated cheese, as long as it is aged and has a sharp flavor. Cutting out the crackers in rounds adds time to this recipe, but the crackers do look beautiful. If you are pressed for time, use the shaping technique used in Sea Salt Crackers (page 73) instead. MAKES ABOUT 8 DOZEN CRACKERS

# PARMIGIANO-REGGIANO CHEESE CRACKERS

¼ cup (60 g) water

2 tablespoons unsalted butter, melted

¼ teaspoon fine sea salt, plus more for sprinkling

½ cup (50 g) grated Parmigiano-Reggiano cheese

¼ teaspoon baking powder

1¼ cups (150 g) all-purpose einkorn flour

**1** Add 1½ inches of water to a baking dish and place on the bottom rack of your oven. Place a rimmed baking sheet on the center rack. Preheat the oven to 400°F.

**2** In a large bowl, mix together the water with the melted butter and salt with a fork until combined. Add the cheese and continue to mix until thick and creamy. Stir in the baking powder. Add the flour and continue to mix with a fork as much as you can, then use your hands to knead the dough in the bowl until it holds together. Rub the dough against the sides of the bowl to collect any remaining flour, then turn it out onto your work surface and knead by hand about 20 times until smooth. Divide the dough into 5 equal pieces, and cover with plastic wrap to keep moist.

**3** Cut a piece of parchment paper to fit your baking sheet. Roll out the first piece of dough as thin as possible on the paper, lifting frequently, until you have a 10-inch round. Sprinkle the surface lightly with salt. Cut out the crackers with a 2-inch round cookie cutter as closely as possible. Pull up the outline of the dough, leaving the round cutouts on the paper. Slide the paper onto the preheated baking sheet. Save the scraps to reroll and make an additional sheet of crackers.

**4** Bake for 8 to 9 minutes until the crackers are lightly golden. Remove the pan from the oven. Lift up the paper and shake the crackers into a large serving bowl to cool. Return the tray to the oven to warm up, then proceed to roll, season, and bake the remaining pieces of dough in the same manner. The crackers can be stored at room temperature in an airtight container for up to 3 days.

THESE SIMPLE 100 PERCENT whole grain crackers are extra delicious. They bake up crispy thanks to a few simple steps. Like with Sea Salt Crackers (page 73) and Parmigiano-Reggiano Cheese Crackers (page 74), it is important to work in small batches so you can roll out the dough as thin as possible. Preheating your baking tray and creating steam in the oven enables the crackers to spring up quickly and bake faster without burning. MAKES ABOUT 9 DOZEN CRACKERS

# WHOLE WHEAT THINS

2 cups (192 g) whole grain einkorn flour

¾ teaspoon fine sea salt, plus more for sprinkling

¼ teaspoon baking powder

2 tablespoons cold unsalted butter, cut into pieces

1 tablespoon extra-virgin olive oil or vegetable oil

1 tablespoon honey

¼ cup (60 g) water

1 Add 1½ inches of water to a baking dish and place on the bottom rack of your oven. Place a rimmed baking sheet on the center rack. Preheat the oven to 400°F.

2 In a large bowl, combine the flour, salt, and baking powder. Cut the butter into the flour using a pastry blender until the mixture has a fine and sandy texture.

3 In a small bowl, whisk together the oil, honey, and water until emulsified. Add the liquid to the dough mixture and squeeze the dough in your hands until it holds together. Turn out to a clean work surface and knead with your hands for about 2 minutes until the dough is still moist, but not sticky.

4 Break off one third of the dough and roll it out on a piece of parchment paper that fits your baking sheet until it is as thin as possible—you should have a 10-inch square. Trim the edges with a pizza or pastry wheel

to form a perfect square, setting the scraps back in the bowl. Prick the dough all over with a fork in even rows. Sprinkle very lightly with salt. Cut the rectangle into 2-inch rows vertically and horizontally to form 25 squares.

5 Slide the paper onto the preheated baking sheet. Save the scraps to reroll and make additional sheets of crackers.

6 Bake for 7 to 8 minutes until the crackers are lightly golden in the center and some of the outer edges have browned considerably. Remove the pan from the oven. Lift up the paper and shake the crackers into a large serving bowl to cool. Return the tray to the oven to warm up, then proceed to roll, season, and bake the remaining pieces of dough in the same manner. The crackers can be stored at room temperature in an airtight container for up to 3 days.

# QUICK BREADS
# & BREAKFAST

**I BELIEVE ALL BREAKFAST FOODS TASTE BETTER WITH EINKORN,** and if you would like to test my theory, start out by making a basic pancake. Whether you mix up a batter with whole grain or all-purpose einkorn flour, you will really notice the delightful flavor einkorn lends to the simplest recipes. The added nutrients will also keep you feeling full for longer, so you can elude those mid-morning bouts of hunger.

I love all of the recipes in this chapter, but my two favorites are Overnight Kefir Coffee Cake (page 96) and Slow-Fermented Belgian Waffles (page 105). You mix up both recipes before going to bed, as they contain ingredients like kefir and buttermilk that will help ferment the dough slowly. This type of preparation is really suited to einkorn because it gives it a long time to completely absorb the liquids and bake up lighter in the morning.

When life presents a challenge, I always think about how wonderful it would be to go back to yesterday's breakfast—a hot cup of tea, a bowl of porridge, feeling the warmth of the kitchen and my family nearby. I often wake up very early and prepare something special for the table, just as my parents did for me. I am really excited that ancient grain einkorn will also be a part of your special mornings.

YOU CAN REALLY TASTE the lovely flavor of einkorn in this simple scone recipe. To achieve the perfect texture after baking, you will find the dough to be tacky while rolling. Do not add more flour and don't be concerned about the roughness of the dough—the scones will correct themselves while baking. I have cut the scones into wedges and given you options for both large and small scones, but you may also use a cookie cutter for round scones. You can add ¼ cup currants here if you like—simply toss them in before adding the cream. MAKES 8 LARGE OR 12 SMALL SCONES

# CLASSIC CREAM SCONES

3 cups (360 g) all-purpose einkorn flour, plus more for dusting

¼ cup (50 g) sugar, plus 1 tablespoon for dusting

1 tablespoon baking powder

¾ teaspoon fine sea salt

10 tablespoons (140 g) cold unsalted butter, cut into ¼-inch cubes

¾ cup (180 g) plus 2 teaspoons cold heavy cream

1 Preheat the oven to 425°F.

2 Mix together the flour, ¼ cup sugar, baking powder, and salt in a large bowl. Work in the butter with your fingers or a pastry blender until the mixture resembles coarse meal but still has some larger chunks of butter. Pour in the ¾ cup cream and squeeze the dough through your hands until the dough barely holds together. Knead the ball of dough 5 to 10 times until the flour is absorbed but the dough is very shaggy, not smooth.

3 Lightly flour a piece of parchment paper and transfer the dough to it. Dust the top of the dough and place another piece of parchment paper on top of the dough. For large scones, use a rolling pin to roll the dough into an 8-inch circle that is ¾ inch

thick. Cut the circle into 8 triangles with a sharp knife. For small scones, use a rolling pin to roll the dough into a 6 × 9-inch rectangle that is 1 inch thick. Cut the rectangle in thirds lengthwise and then in half crosswise. Cut each rectangle in half diagonally for 12 small wedges.

4 Line a baking sheet with parchment paper and place the scones on it, spaced about 1½ inches apart. Brush the tops of the scones with the 2 teaspoons cream and dust with the remaining 1 tablespoon of sugar. Bake for 18 to 20 minutes until lightly golden.

5 Remove the scones with a metal spatula to a plate and serve warm, or let cool before serving. Store in a sealed plastic bag for up to 2 days, or freeze for up to 1 month.

**THESE WONDERFUL RUSTIC SCONES** are embellished with bright red strawberries. I use a little bit more whole grain than all-purpose einkorn flour in this recipe and augment the butter with mascarpone cheese. Don't worry too much about getting the dough to look perfect, as it will bubble up, expand, and correct itself in the oven. If you can't find mascarpone, you can substitute sour cream or crème fraîche. MAKES 8 LARGE OR 12 SMALL SCONES

# FRESH STRAWBERRY MASCARPONE SCONES

2 cups (192 g) whole grain einkorn flour

1½ cups (180 g) all-purpose einkorn flour

½ cup (100 g) plus 2 tablespoons sugar

1 tablespoon baking powder

½ teaspoon fine sea salt

8 tablespoons (114 g) cold unsalted butter, cut into ¼-inch cubes

¾ cup (170 g) cold mascarpone cheese

2 cups (288 g) large fresh strawberries, diced

**1** Preheat the oven to 425°F.

**2** Mix the flours, the ½ cup sugar, the baking powder, and the salt in a large bowl. Work in the butter with your fingers or a pastry blender until the mixture resembles coarse meal but still has some large chunks of butter throughout.

**3** Add the mascarpone to the flour mixture and mix by squeezing the dough between your hands until it just begins to hold together and there is barely any dry flour visible. Gather half of the dough into a ball and place between 2 pieces of parchment paper.

**4** For large scones, use a rolling pin to roll the dough to an 8-inch round that is about ¼ inch thick. Spread three quarters of the strawberries on the dough, reaching to the edges. Dust with 1 tablespoon sugar.

On a new piece of parchment paper, roll the remaining dough to an 8-inch round and flip on top of the strawberry-covered dough. Using your fingers, gently seal the edges of the two dough rounds. Place the remaining diced strawberries on top, pressing down gently to just rest in place. Dust with the remaining 1 tablespoon sugar. Cut the circle into 8 wedges with a sharp knife.

**5** For small scones, use a rolling pin to roll half the dough into a 6 × 9-inch rectangle that is about ¼ inch thick. Spread three quarters of the strawberries on the dough, reaching to the edges. Dust with 1 tablespoon of sugar. On a new piece of parchment paper, roll the remaining dough to a 6 × 9-inch rectangle and flip on top of the strawberry-covered dough. Using your fingers, gently seal the edges of the 2 dough rectangles. Top with the rest of the strawberries and gently press them

into the dough. Dust with the remaining 1 tablespoon sugar. Cut the rectangle in thirds lengthwise and then in half crosswise. Cut each rectangle in half diagonally to form 12 small wedges.

**6** Line a baking sheet with parchment paper. Lift the scones with a metal spatula and place them on the baking sheet, spaced about 2 inches apart.

**7** Bake the scones for 20 to 22 minutes until deeply golden around the edges. Let the scones cool on the baking tray for 15 minutes. Remove the scones with a metal spatula to a plate and serve warm, or let cool before serving. Store in a sealed plastic bag for up to 2 days, or freeze for up to 1 month.

**THE TASTE OF PEANUT** butter and jelly resonates with everyone around me, and you'll find that peanuts combine well with the nutty flavor of whole grain einkorn flour. You may also convert this recipe to a classic whole grain scone by substituting the peanut butter and milk with ¾ cup of heavy cream, and omit the peanuts and preserves. MAKES 8 LARGE OR 12 SMALL SCONES

# WHOLE GRAIN PEANUT BUTTER & JELLY SCONES

3¾ cups (360 g) whole grain einkorn flour

¼ cup (55 g) (packed) dark brown sugar

1 tablespoon baking powder

¾ teaspoon fine sea salt

10 tablespoons (140 g) cold unsalted butter, cut into ¼-inch cubes

½ cup (75 g) roasted peanuts

½ cup (122 g) whole milk, plus 1 teaspoon for brushing

⅓ cup (86 g) creamy natural peanut butter

⅓ cup (80 g) strawberry preserves

1 tablespoon granulated sugar, for dusting

**1** Preheat the oven to 425°F.

**2** Mix the flour, brown sugar, baking powder, and salt in a large bowl. Work in the butter with your fingers or a pastry blender until the mixture resembles coarse meal but still has some large chunks of butter throughout. Mix in the peanuts.

**3** In a small bowl, whisk together the ½ cup milk and the peanut butter with a fork. Add to the flour mixture and mix in the bowl by squeezing the dough between your hands until the dough holds together in a sticky ball.

**4** Gather half of the dough into a ball, then flatten into a disk.

**5** Gather the other half of the dough into a ball and use a rolling pin to roll between 2 pieces of parchment paper to a 6 × 9-inch rectangle that is about ¼ inch thick. If the dough sticks to the rolling pin, dust the rolling pin lightly with flour. Spread the strawberry preserves on top of the round to about 1 inch from the edges. On a new piece of parchment paper, roll the remaining dough to a 6 × 9-inch rectangle and flip on top of the preserve-covered dough. Using your fingers, gently seal the edges. Brush the top with the remaining 1 teaspoon milk and dust with the granulated sugar. Cut the circle into 8 large wedges with a sharp knife, or cut the rectangle in thirds lengthwise and then in half

crosswise, and then cut each rectangle in half diagonally to form 12 small wedges. Line a baking sheet with parchment paper. Lift the scones with a metal spatula and place them on the baking sheet, spaced about 1½ inches apart.

**6** Bake the scones for 18 minutes until golden brown. Remove the scones with a metal spatula to a plate and let cool slightly before serving.

**THIS IS A SAVORY** quick bread with antipasto flavors tucked inside—olives, salami, ham, and specialty cheeses—and can be served any time of the day. Once you have the recipe down, you can change the antipasto ingredients for new flavor combinations. The batter will be thicker than a normal quick bread, but it will keep the savory ingredients suspended in the dough. Expect this bread to darken considerably on the top during baking. MAKES 1 LOAF

# SAVORY ANTIPASTO QUICK BREAD

2 cups (240 g) all-purpose einkorn flour

2½ teaspoons baking powder

½ teaspoon fine sea salt

⅓ cup (50 g) grated pecorino Romano cheese

¼ teaspoon dried oregano

2 large eggs

½ cup (122 g) whole milk

¼ cup (50 g) extra-virgin olive oil, plus more for greasing the pan

2 tablespoons dry white wine

1 cup (130 g) diced firm cheese, such as Manchego, Swiss, or Colby

½ cup (60 g) diced salami or mortadella

½ cup (60 g) diced ham or turkey

½ cup (60 g) pitted and sliced green olives

**1** Preheat the oven to 375°F. Grease a 9 × 5-inch loaf pan.

**2** In a large mixing bowl, sift together the flour, baking powder, and salt. Mix in the pecorino cheese and oregano.

**3** In a medium bowl, whisk the eggs until foamy. Whisk in the milk, oil, and wine until combined.

**4** Fold the egg mixture into the flour mixture, and use a spatula to mix until the flour is completely absorbed. Add the diced cheese, meats, and olives, mixing them into the batter evenly with a fork. Transfer the batter into the prepared loaf pan.

**5** Bake the bread for 40 to 45 minutes until a toothpick comes out clean in the center. Let the bread cool in the pan for 15 minutes, then unmold the bread and let cool completely on a rack before slicing.

**WHEN LEAF LARD IS** derived from pasture-raised pigs, it is a healthy baking fat. It has nearly one fourth the saturated fat and more than twice the monounsaturated fat as butter. Leaf lard gives biscuits the most tender and flaky texture, and the added butter lends a nice flavor. Alternatively, you can substitute the lard with bacon fat, or use all butter, in these cheesy biscuits, which are filled with the smoky flavor of bacon. MAKES 10 BISCUITS

# BACON & CHEDDAR BUTTERMILK BISCUITS

8 ounces (226 g) thin-sliced bacon

2½ cups (300 g) all-purpose einkorn flour, plus more for dusting

1 tablespoon baking powder

¼ teaspoon baking soda

½ teaspoon fine sea salt

4 tablespoons (55 g) cold unsalted butter, cut into ¼-inch cubes

2 tablespoons (25 g) cold leaf lard

1 cup (115 g) shredded sharp Cheddar cheese

½ cup (124 g) cold buttermilk

**1** Preheat the oven to 350°F.

**2** Arrange the bacon on a broiler pan or on a wire rack set over a baking sheet. Cook for 10 minutes until the bacon is just brown around the edges; do not let the bacon crisp, or it will be dry in your biscuits. Set aside to cool until you can handle it, then cut the slices into bite-size pieces. Raise the oven temperature to 425°F.

**3** Mix the flour, baking powder, baking soda, and salt in a large bowl. Work in the butter and lard with your fingers or a pastry blender until the mixture resembles coarse meal but still has some larger chunks of butter. Add the bacon pieces and ¾ cup of the cheese and press into the dough evenly.

Add the buttermilk and squeeze the dough through your hands until it begins to hold together in a ball.

**4** Lightly dust a sheet of parchment paper with flour and transfer the dough to it. Dust the top of the dough lightly with flour. Use a rolling pin to roll the dough into an 8 × 12-inch rectangle. Fold the dough in thirds, scraping and adding back any dough that has stuck to the paper. Press the dough together to form a 4 × 6-inch rectangle. Roll the dough into a 6 × 8-inch rectangle that is 1 inch thick. Use a 3-inch round cookie cutter to cut out rounds as closely together as possible and without turning while cutting the dough. Gather the remaining dough, press to 1-inch thickness, and continue to cut out the biscuits until all the dough is used.

Sprinkle the remaining ¼ cup cheese on top of the biscuits and transfer to a parchment-lined baking sheet.

**5** Bake the biscuits for 18 to 20 minutes until the bottoms are golden and the biscuits are cooked through. Let cool slightly before removing from the baking sheet. Serve warm or at room temperature.

**IF YOU HAVE BAKED** muffins with einkorn in the past, you probably enjoyed the nice flavor but might have found the texture a bit denser than what you wanted. Instead of supporting large bubbles and a light texture, einkorn tends to rise evenly and create a denser crumb. But if you modify your mixing techniques, you can create a moist and tender texture. You should let the flour hydrate in the acidic liquids and whip the eggs with sugar until they become creamy and thick, giving strength to the structure of the muffin. Here you have a perfect basic einkorn muffin batter—I've added blueberries, but you may substitute any seasonal fresh, frozen, or dried fruit and nuts as you like. I have found that preheating to a higher temperature and then lowering the temperature once the muffins go in the oven gives them a much-needed spring, resulting in a nice shape and lighter texture. MAKES 12 MUFFINS

# YOGURT BLUEBERRY MUFFINS

3 cups (360 g) all-purpose einkorn flour, plus 1 teaspoon for dusting

2 teaspoons baking powder

½ teaspoon baking soda

½ teaspoon fine sea salt

¾ cup (185 g) plain yogurt

½ cup (125 g) whole milk

10 tablespoons (140 g) unsalted butter, melted

3 large eggs

1 cup (200 g) sugar

2 cups (240 g) fresh or frozen blueberries

**1** Preheat the oven to 425°F. Fill a muffin tin with 12 paper liners.

**2** In a large mixing bowl, sift together the 3 cups (360 g) flour, baking powder, baking soda, and salt. In a medium bowl, combine the yogurt, milk, and melted butter.

**3** In the bowl of a standing mixer fitted with a wire whip attachment, beat the eggs until they are a smooth yellow color. Add the sugar and beat on medium-low speed for 1 minute, then on high for 4 minutes until the mixture forms thick ribbons.

**4** Fold the flour mixture gently into the egg, using a circular motion to completely incorporate it into the batter. Gently stir

the yogurt mixture into the batter. (Be sure to scrape the sides and bottom of the bowl as you go.) Toss the blueberries with the remaining 1 teaspoon flour, then fold them gently into the batter until the dry flour is completely absorbed. Spoon the batter evenly into the cups, filling nearly to the rim of the cup.

**5** Place the muffins in the oven, then reduce the oven temperature to 375°F. Bake for 30 minutes until a toothpick comes away clean when inserted in the center of the muffins. Let cool in the pan for 15 minutes, then remove from the pan and cool completely. The muffins can be stored in an airtight container for up to 3 days.

BY USING THE SAME mixing technique as for Yogurt Blueberry Muffins (page 91) and changing up some of the ingredients, you'll have another great einkorn muffin for breakfast or to take on the go. I've used sour cream instead of yogurt, added a bit of whole grain flour, and topped the muffins with walnut streusel. MAKES 12 MUFFINS

# CINNAMON WALNUT STREUSEL MUFFINS

FOR THE STREUSEL TOPPING

¼ cup (30 g) all-purpose einkorn flour

2 tablespoons (30 g) sugar

½ teaspoon ground cinnamon

Pinch of fine sea salt

3 tablespoons (40 g) cold unsalted butter, cut into ¼-inch cubes

½ cup (60 g) chopped walnuts

FOR THE MUFFIN BATTER

2 cups (240 g) all-purpose einkorn flour

1⅓ cups (128 g) whole grain einkorn flour

2 teaspoons ground cinnamon

2 teaspoons baking powder

½ teaspoon baking soda

½ teaspoon sea salt

⅔ cup (162 g) whole milk

½ cup (120 g) sour cream

8 tablespoons (113 g) unsalted butter, melted

3 large eggs

1 cup (200 g) sugar

1 Preheat the oven to 425°F. Fill a muffin tin with 12 paper liners.

2 MAKE THE STREUSEL: Mix together the flour, sugar, cinnamon, and salt in a medium bowl. Work the butter into the flour mixture with a pastry cutter or your hands until the chunks are thoroughly cut into the flour. Sprinkle in the walnuts and stir to combine. Refrigerate while you prepare the muffin batter.

3 MAKE THE MUFFIN BATTER: In a large bowl, sift together the flours, cinnamon, baking powder, baking soda, and salt. In a medium bowl, combine the milk, sour cream, and butter.

4 Add the eggs to the bowl of a standing mixer fitted with a wire whip attachment, and blend to combine into a smooth yellow mixture. Add the sugar and beat on medium-low speed for 1 minute, then on high for 4 minutes, until the mixture forms thick ribbons.

**5** Fold the flour mixture into the eggs; using a circular motion to completely incorporate it into the batter. Gently stir the milk mixture into the batter. (Be sure to scrape the sides and bottom of the bowl as you go.) Don't overmix—it is fine if the batter seems to have small clumps of flour throughout.

**6** Spoon the batter evenly into the cups, filling nearly to the rim of the cup. Sprinkle the streusel evenly on top of the muffins.

**7** Place the muffins in the oven, then lower the oven temperature to 375°F. Bake for 25 minutes until a toothpick comes away clean when inserted in the center of the muffins. Let cool in the pan for 15 minutes, then lift out the muffins and let cool completely. The muffins can be stored in an airtight container for up to 3 days.

**AS WHOLE GRAIN EINKORN** bakers, we've got quite an advantage over our modern wheat-baking friends. It's the pleasingly nutty flavor of ancient einkorn that gives us a sweet-tasting whole grain flavor that does not taste gritty or overbearing. In this yummy muffin recipe, I've cut the sugar in the batter, added a few spoonfuls of honey and raisins, and then topped the muffins with a silken honey and powdered sugar glaze. MAKES 12 MUFFINS

# HONEY-GLAZED WHOLE GRAIN RAISIN MUFFINS

FOR THE MUFFIN BATTER

1 cup (135 g) raisins

4 cups (384 g) whole grain einkorn flour

2½ teaspoons baking powder

½ teaspoon baking soda

½ teaspoon fine sea salt

3 large eggs

½ cup (110 g) (packed) dark brown sugar

1⅓ cups (327 g) buttermilk

4 tablespoons (56 g) unsalted butter, melted

¼ cup (50 g) extra-virgin olive oil or vegetable oil

2 tablespoons honey

FOR THE GLAZE

¾ cup (90 g) powdered sugar, sifted

2 teaspoons honey

**1** Preheat the oven to 425°F. Fill a muffin tin with 12 paper liners.

**2** MAKE THE MUFFIN BATTER: Combine the raisins and ¼ cup (59 g) of boiling water in a small bowl to soak and soften for 15 minutes. Drain the raisins and squeeze out any excess soaking water.

**3** In a large mixing bowl, sift together the flour, baking powder, baking soda, and salt.

**4** In a standing mixer, blend the eggs together until you have a smooth yellow mixture. Add the brown sugar and beat on medium-low speed for 1 minute, then on high for 4 minutes, until the mixture forms thick ribbons.

**5** In a medium bowl, stir together the buttermilk, butter, oil, and honey.

**6** Fold the flour mixture into the eggs, using a circular motion to completely incorporate it into the batter. Gently stir the buttermilk mixture into the batter. (Be sure to scrape the sides and bottom of the bowl as you go.) Fold in the raisins. Spoon the batter evenly into the cups, filling to the rim.

**7** Place the muffins in the oven and lower the temperature to 375°F. Bake for 25 minutes, rotating the muffin pan halfway through the cooking time, until a toothpick comes away clean when inserted in the center of the muffins. Let cool in the pan for 15 minutes, then lift the muffins out and let cool on a wire rack for 10 minutes more before glazing.

**8** **MAKE THE GLAZE:** In a small bowl, mix together the sugar and honey, then stir in 2 teaspoons water until the mixture is creamy. Spread 1 scant teaspoon of the glaze on each muffin using the back of a spoon. The muffins can be stored in an airtight container for up to 3 days.

**KEFIR IS A FERMENTED** milk product similar to yogurt but with the consistency of a thinner liquid; it contains three times more healthful probiotics than regular yogurt. The beneficial yeasts in kefir will work slowly in the refrigerator overnight to leaven the batter, so this lovely coffee cake will have a deliciously light crumb. This recipe turned out great the first time I made it and has been perfect every time since. MAKES ONE 9 × 13-INCH CAKE

# OVERNIGHT KEFIR COFFEE CAKE

FOR THE CAKE

2½ cups (300 g) all-purpose einkorn flour, plus more for dusting

2 teaspoons baking powder

½ teaspoon baking soda

½ teaspoon fine sea salt

10 tablespoons (140 g) unsalted butter, at room temperature, plus more for greasing the baking dish

½ cup (100 g) granulated sugar

½ cup (110 g) (packed) dark brown sugar

3 large eggs

½ teaspoon pure vanilla extract

1 cup (240 g) kefir

FOR THE CRUMB TOPPING

¾ cup (90 g) all-purpose einkorn flour

¼ cup (50 g) granulated sugar

¼ teaspoon fine sea salt

6 tablespoons (84 g) cold unsalted butter, cut into ¼-inch cubes

¼ teaspoon ground cinnamon

¼ teaspoon unsweetened cocoa powder

Powdered sugar, for dusting

**1** MAKE THE CAKE: Sift together the flour, baking powder, baking soda, and salt in a medium bowl.

**2** In the bowl of a standing mixer fitted with the paddle attachment, cream the butter on medium-low speed for 2 to 3 minutes. Add the sugars and mix on medium-low for 1 to 2 minutes until the butter is fluffy and whipped. Add the eggs and vanilla and mix on medium-low until just combined, scraping down the sides and bottom of the bowl. Detach the bowl from the mixer.

**3** Use a spatula to fold half of the flour mixture into the egg mixture. Fold in ½ cup of the kefir, then repeat with the remaining flour mixture and kefir until everything is just combined. (Do not overwork the batter.) Cover the bowl with plastic wrap and store in the refrigerator all night or up to 8 hours.

**4** When you are ready to bake, butter and flour a 9 × 13-inch baking dish. Preheat the oven to 350°F.

**5** Remove the batter from the refrigerator and spread it out into the prepared dish. Set aside.

**6** **MAKE THE TOPPING:** Mix together the flour, granulated sugar, and salt in a medium bowl. Cut the butter into the flour mixture with a pastry blender until the butter is completely incorporated into the flour in small chunks. The topping can be made at night and stored in the refrigerator with the cake batter.

**7** Sprinkle half of the mixture on top of the cake. In a small bowl, combine the cinnamon and cocoa powder and sprinkle evenly over the topping. Sprinkle the remaining topping over the cinnamon and cocoa. Bake for 42 minutes until the middle springs back when pressed with your finger.

**8** Let the cake sit in the pan for 1 hour until completely cooled. Dust with powdered sugar and serve.

**WHEN YOUR KITCHEN FILLS** with the aroma of bananas simmering in coconut oil and brown sugar, everyone in your house will know it's time for banana bread. What makes this bread even better is that we can benefit from the sweetness of the ripe bananas and reduce the amount of added sugar. My mom made delicious banana bread when I was a child, but I can't help but think about how lucky my children are that they get to eat theirs made with einkorn. I hope you feel the same excitement about baking this quick bread for your loved ones. MAKES 1 LOAF

# WHOLE GRAIN CARAMELIZED BANANA BREAD

**FOR THE BREAD**

2½ cups (240 g) whole grain einkorn flour

1 teaspoon baking soda

½ teaspoon fine sea salt

5 tablespoons (65 g) extra-virgin coconut oil, plus more for greasing the pan

3 very ripe bananas, cut into ½-inch slices

½ cup (105 g) (packed) dark brown sugar

3 large eggs

**FOR THE GLAZE**

½ cup (60 g) powdered sugar

Pinch of ground cinnamon

Pinch of ground ginger

**1** Preheat the oven to 350°F. Grease a 4½ × 8½-inch loaf pan.

**2** MAKE THE BREAD: In a large bowl, sift together the flour, baking soda, and salt.

**3** In a medium skillet, heat the coconut oil until it melts. Add the bananas and brown sugar. Simmer on medium-low heat for 5 minutes, stirring occasionally, until the bananas have softened and the sugar begins to caramelize. Allow the bananas to cool for 10 minutes.

**4** Combine the bananas and eggs in a blender or food processor, and process to a smooth purée. Fold the banana mixture into the

flour with a spatula until just combined. Pour the batter into the loaf pan.

**5** Bake the bread for 42 minutes until a toothpick comes away clean when inserted in the center of the bread. Let the bread cool in the pan for 10 minutes, then unmold the loaf and let cool on a rack for 30 minutes before glazing.

**6** MAKE THE GLAZE: Combine the powdered sugar, cinnamon, and ginger in a small bowl. Add 2 teaspoons water and mix until the sugar dissolves. Spread on the top of the bread.

**7** Store at room temperature, covered with plastic wrap, for up to 3 days.

**IN ORDER TO HAVE** consistent results with zucchini bread, especially when made with einkorn flour, it is important to reduce the moisture in the zucchini. To do this, I use a technique that is often used in Italy for preparing zucchini for frying. Salt will draw the water out of the vegetable, so you can then squeeze out the excess. This allows you to add more zucchini to your bread. I like to keep this recipe very simple so I can taste the flavor of the zucchini and the nice combination of whole grain and all-purpose einkorn flour. MAKES 1 LOAF

# ZUCCHINI BREAD

2 cups (200 g) shredded zucchini (from 1 to 2 medium zucchini)

½ teaspoon plus ¼ teaspoon fine sea salt

⅔ cup (133 g) extra-virgin olive oil, plus more for greasing the pan

1 cup (120 g) all-purpose einkorn flour

1 cup (96 g) whole grain einkorn flour

1½ teaspoons baking powder

½ teaspoon baking soda

2 large eggs

¾ cup (150 g) granulated sugar

¼ cup (55 g) packed dark brown sugar

**1** Mix the zucchini with ½ teaspoon salt and place in a fine mesh strainer. Let stand for 15 minutes. Squeeze the zucchini to extract as much water as possible.

**2** Preheat the oven to 350°F. Grease an 8½ × 4½-inch loaf pan.

**3** In a medium bowl, sift together the flours, baking powder, baking soda, and the remaining ¼ teaspoon salt.

**4** In a large bowl, whisk together the eggs, sugars, and ⅔ cup oil. Stir in the zucchini. Working 1 cup at a time, stir the flour mixture into the wet ingredients, and gently whisk until all of the flour is absorbed. (Do not overmix.) Pour the batter into the prepared loaf pan.

**5** Bake the bread for 52 minutes until a toothpick comes out clean in the center. Let cool in the pan for 5 minutes, then unmold the bread and let cool on a cooling rack before serving.

**EINKORN WHEAT BERRIES ARE** sweet and nutty and I love to add a bit of the cracked berries to my pancake batter to add an irresistible chewy texture. The extra protein in the whole einkorn grain will sustain you much longer than pancakes made with regular wheat flour. MAKES 12 TO 15 PANCAKES

# WHOLE GRAIN EINKORN PANCAKES

¼ cup (50 g) einkorn wheat berries

⅛ teaspoon plus ¼ teaspoon fine sea salt

2 tablespoons unsalted butter, melted, plus more for greasing the griddle

2 large eggs

1 cup (244 g) whole milk

½ cup (122 g) plain yogurt

2 cups (192 g) whole grain einkorn flour

¼ cup (26 g) golden flax meal

2 tablespoons (packed) light brown sugar

2 teaspoons baking powder

Pure maple syrup, for serving

**1** Use a food processor, blender, or grain mill to crack the einkorn wheat berries. The endosperm or interior of the grain will be very fine, but the outer shell should just crack into medium pieces.

**2** In a small saucepan, bring ¾ cup water to a boil. Whisk in the ⅛ teaspoon salt and the cracked wheat berries. Simmer, covered, on low heat for 20 minutes. Remove from the heat, add the butter, then cover and let stand for 10 minutes.

**3** Whisk together the eggs, milk, and yogurt in a large mixing bowl.

**4** In a medium bowl, combine the flour, flax meal, brown sugar, baking powder, and the remaining ¼ teaspoon salt. Add the flour mixture to the egg mixture and whisk gently until you have a smooth batter. Fold in the cooked wheat berries and melted butter.

**5** Heat your griddle or skillet to medium-low and grease lightly with butter. Scoop ¼ cup of the batter for each pancake onto the griddle and cook for 2 to 3 minutes until the edges are dry and bubbles start to form, then flip the pancake and cook for 1 to 2 minutes until cooked through. The pancakes will expand nicely and cook well inside, but you might not see the same amount of bubbles that you are used to with regular wheat flour, so be careful not to burn the bottom before flipping. Serve with maple syrup.

**I THINK YOU WILL** agree these are the best pancakes you have ever tasted! The delicious flavor of einkorn can really be noted here. The lutein in einkorn flour gives these pancakes a deep golden color. I recommend sifting the flour twice—all-purpose einkorn flour can form clumps easily, as it becomes very fine during milling. If you would like to add blueberries or other fruit, you can gently fold them in once the batter is hydrated. Einkorn flour benefits both in flavor and digestibility if soaked in buttermilk, so you may mix the batter and refrigerate overnight for the lightest pancakes.

MAKES 12 PANCAKES

# GOLDEN BUTTERMILK PANCAKES

1¾ cups (210 g) all-purpose einkorn flour

1 tablespoon sugar

2 teaspoons baking powder

½ teaspoon fine sea salt

¼ teaspoon baking soda

2 large eggs

1½ cups (360 g) buttermilk

2 tablespoons unsalted butter, melted, plus more for frying the pancakes

1 cup fresh or frozen fruit (optional)

Pure maple syrup, for serving

**1** In a medium bowl, sift together the flour, sugar, baking powder, salt, and baking soda.

**2** Whisk together the eggs, buttermilk, and melted butter in a large bowl.

**3** Add the flour mixture to the wet mixture, and whisk briefly but vigorously until the batter is smooth. Add your fruit of choice here, if using.

**4** Heat a skillet or cast-iron griddle to medium-low heat and grease lightly with butter. Scoop up ⅓ cup of batter at a time and pour onto the griddle. Cook for 1 to 2 minutes until the edges are dry and bubbles start to form. Flip the pancakes and cook for another 1 to 2 minutes until cooked through. You might not see the same amount of bubbles that you are used to with regular wheat flour, so be careful not to burn the bottom before flipping. Transfer the cooked pancakes to a plate, then cover and repeat with the remaining pancakes. Serve warm with maple syrup.

MAKE THIS BATTER AFTER dinner and allow it to proof slowly overnight. In the morning, you'll find a bubbly batter that is ready for your waffle iron. Letting your waffles ferment overnight will create a chewy interior and a nice slightly sour flavor. I wanted these waffles to be very crispy and stay that way long after they left the waffle iron, and this is achieved with the addition of heavy cream. If you do not have time for overnight proofing, increase the yeast to 1 teaspoon and let the batter proof at room temperature for 1 to 2 hours before baking. MAKES 6 THICK WAFFLES

# SLOW-FERMENTED BELGIAN WAFFLES

¼ cup (60 g) refreshed Einkorn Sourdough Starter (page 10), or ¼ teaspoon active dry yeast

¼ cup (60 g) warm water at 100°F

1 cup (240 g) buttermilk or kefir

1¼ cups (300 g) whole milk

½ cup (120 g) heavy cream

3 tablespoons extra-virgin olive oil or vegetable oil

4 cups (480 g) all-purpose einkorn flour

2 tablespoons sugar

1 teaspoon fine sea salt

3 large eggs, separated

4 tablespoons (56 g) unsalted butter, melted and cooled

Pure maple syrup, for serving

1 In a large bowl, dissolve the starter or yeast in the water with a fork. Whisk in the buttermilk or kefir, milk, cream, and oil.

2 Sift together the flour, sugar, and salt in a medium bowl. Whisk the dry ingredients into the wet mixture until the batter is smooth. Cover the bowl and let the batter stand at room temperature overnight, or for 6 to 8 hours.

3 Preheat the waffle iron (and grease with butter or oil if your model requires it). Uncover the bowl of batter and whisk in the egg yolks and butter.

4 In the bowl of a standing mixer fitted with a wire whisk attachment, beat the egg whites until soft peaks form, about 3 minutes. Use a rubber spatula to gently fold the egg whites into the waffle batter until just mixed.

5 Spread 1 cup of the batter nearly to the edges of the waffle iron. Bake using a medium-high setting for approximately 4 minutes, or until the waffles are deeply golden and crisp. Serve immediately with maple syrup, or keep warm in the oven preheated to 300°F until ready to serve.

ROLLED EINKORN FLAKES CAN be substituted 1:1 for rolled oats in just about any granola recipe, but because the grain is so much smaller than oats, the small flakes bake up crunchier. Since my children are not lovers of crunchy granola bars, I wanted to create a soft bar that they could easily pack for a snack. These chewy bars are made with healthy nuts, seeds, and dried fruit, and each bar contains roughly 9 grams of protein. Adding a bit of jam will help set up the bars when cooled and lend a fruity sweetness. MAKES 10 TO 12 BARS

# PROTEIN-PACKED SOFT GRANOLA BARS

3 cups (285 g) rolled einkorn flakes (see page 20)

½ teaspoon fine sea salt

1 cup coarsely chopped nuts, such as almonds, walnuts, pecans, or Brazil nuts

¾ cup dried fruit, such as raisins, cranberries, or blueberries

½ cup chocolate chips or shredded coconut

½ cup large seeds, such as pepitas or sunflower seeds

2 tablespoons small seeds, such as flax, sesame, or chia seeds

4 tablespoons (56 g) butter

½ cup (100 g) sugar

¼ cup (40 g) apricot, peach, or strawberry jam

¼ cup (50 g) extra-virgin olive oil

**1** Preheat the oven to 325°F.

**2** Pulse ½ cup (48 g) of the rolled einkorn flakes in a food processor to coarse flour. In a large bowl, stir the ground flakes with the whole flakes, salt, nuts, fruit, chocolate chips or coconut, and large and small seeds.

**3** In a small saucepan, melt the butter on medium-low heat. Stir in the sugar and 1 tablespoon of water and cook for about 1 minute until the sauce begins to bubble and caramelize. Mix in the jam and cook for 1 minute until the mixture begins to thicken. Let stand for 2 minutes to cool.

**4** Add the olive oil to the granola mixture and mix to distribute. Add the sugar mixture and mix until thoroughly combined.

**5** Place a piece of parchment paper on a work surface and turn the granola mixture onto it. Wet your hands and press the granola into a 1-inch-thick rectangle. Use a large knife to push the sides into a rectangle and pat down the top to even it out. Slice the rectangle roughly into 2 x 4-inch bars. Slide the bars with the parchment paper onto a baking sheet.

**6** Bake the granola bars for 30 minutes until browned around the edges. Allow the granola to cool completely on the baking sheet before serving. They can be stored in a sealed airtight container for up to 1 week.

**IT IS BELIEVED THAT** the Romans ground einkorn wheat berries and cooked them to breakfast porridge for strength. A breakfast fit for champions, einkorn porridge is packed with protein, fiber, B vitamins, and trace minerals. To fully reap the benefits of this superfood, proper preparation is important. Soak the wheat berries overnight, then drain and rinse in the morning. Drop them in the food processor and pulse until the grains are chopped coarsely. When cooked, the wheat berries will already have a perfectly sweet and nutty flavor. Serving suggestions are endless really—maple syrup, honey, cream, milk, applesauce, jam, butter, dried fruit, or nuts. My husband eats his porridge with a drizzle of jovial extra-virgin olive oil, but really, he puts olive oil on everything!

SERVES 4

# BREAKFAST PORRIDGE

1½ cups (300 g) einkorn wheat berries

½ teaspoon salt

**1** Soak the wheat berries in 3 cups of water overnight. In the morning, drain the wheat berries in a fine mesh strainer. Rinse thoroughly with cold water and let drain for 5 minutes.

**2** Add the wheat berries to a food processor. Pulse until the wheat has cracked, meaning the wheat berries are no longer in whole pieces but resemble rough steel cut oats. Add 1 cup of water and process for 30 seconds until the mixture is coarse and creamy.

**3** In a medium saucepan, bring 5 cups of water to a boil. Add the salt and wheat berry mixture. Return to a boil, stirring constantly, then lower the heat to a simmer. Cover and cook for 12 minutes, stirring occasionally.

**4** Turn off the heat and let stand, covered, for 10 minutes. Serve warm. The porridge may be stored in an airtight container in the refrigerator for up to 3 days and reheated with added water and milk, if needed.

# COOKIES & CAKES

ALMOND SUGAR COOKIES

GOODNESS GRAHAM
CRACKERS

SOFT & CHEWY GINGER
COOKIES

"OATMEAL"-FLAX SULTANAS
COOKIES

OLIVE OIL & WINE COOKIES

CHOCOLATE CHIP COOKIES

SPONGE CAKE WITH
STRAWBERRIES &
MASCARPONE CREAM

CLASSIC CARROT CAKE

DAIRY-FREE COCONUT
POUND CAKE

VANILLA CUPCAKES WITH
STRAWBERRY CREAM CHEESE
FROSTING

CHOCOLATE CUPCAKES
WITH CHOCOLATE CHIP
BUTTERCREAM FROSTING

WHOLE GRAIN BUNDT CAKE
WITH RUM CARAMEL GLAZE

FUDGY DARK CHOCOLATE
BROWNIES

BROOKLYN BLACKOUT CAKE

THIS CHAPTER IS FULL OF THE CLASSIC FAVORITES THAT every American family wants in their arsenal: graham crackers, chocolate chip cookies, brownies, carrot cake, cupcakes, and more. Baking cookies with einkorn actually takes a bit of getting used to because einkorn not only absorbs liquids slowly, but like gluten-free flours, it also absorbs less fat than modern wheat. Since cookies are high in fat, you have to find the right balance between flour and butter. Too much butter, and the cookies will spread and crisp up. Too much flour will give you a cakey texture and a less decadent cookie. Cookie recipes that contain melted fats, like Soft & Chewy Ginger Cookies (page 117) and "Oatmeal"-Flax Sultanas Cookies (page 118), are what einkorn likes best.

The cake recipes call for sifting and folding, and sometimes sifting twice. The einkorn grain is small and softer than regular wheat owing to how the endosperm breaks down when the grain is milled into flour. When folding einkorn flour in cake batters, expect the flour to stay suspended in the batter and resist absorption. Continue to move your spatula gently in a circular motion, working from the bottom of the bowl upward.

There are three recipes containing chocolate in this chapter: Fudgy Dark Chocolate Brownies (page 136), Chocolate Cupcakes with Chocolate Chip Buttercream Frosting (page 132), and Brooklyn Blackout Cake (page 137). In my experience, einkorn recipes with chocolate come out lighter when I use cocoa powder exclusively or in combination with bakers' chocolate, because einkorn has such difficulty absorbing the fat in chocolate. In all of my recipes, I have left spices and flavorings at a minimum, especially vanilla extract, because I want you to really taste the flavor of einkorn, even as you make these sweet treats.

**THE FIRST TIME I** made sugar cookies with einkorn, I almost cried. I had fourteen co-workers coming over for a holiday party and was trying to make cookies, but the dough was so sticky, it was impossible to roll out. Having learned so much about this flour, I thought it would be easy to convert any recipe. But then I realized I needed to add more flour until the dough was manageable, and the finished cookies turned out delicious. With einkorn, it is always about striking the perfect balance between manageability of the dough and the right baking ratios of flour to fat or liquid. I like to add almond flour to these cookies, but I also bake them without by omitting the almond flour and making no other adjustments. MAKES TWENTY-FOUR 2½-INCH COOKIES

# ALMOND SUGAR COOKIES

2¼ cups (270 g) all-purpose einkorn flour, plus more for dusting

½ cup (50 g) almond flour

1 teaspoon baking powder

⅛ teaspoon sea salt

8 tablespoons (113 g) unsalted butter, at room temperature

¾ cup (150 g) granulated sugar

1 large egg

1 tablespoon whole milk yogurt

¼ teaspoon pure vanilla extract

**1** Preheat the oven to 375°F. Line a baking sheet with parchment paper or a silicone mat.

**2** In a medium bowl, stir together the flours, baking powder, and salt.

**3** Cream together the butter and the granulated sugar for 2 minutes in the bowl of a standing mixer fitted with the paddle attachment on medium-low speed, stopping a few times to scrape down the sides. Add the egg, yogurt, and vanilla and mix for 1 minute until thoroughly combined. Add the flour mixture and mix on low speed until just incorporated, scraping down the sides. Wrap the dough in plastic wrap and refrigerate for 30 minutes to 1 hour.

**4** Working with half of the dough at a time, dust a piece of parchment paper and the dough with flour. Roll the dough to ¼ inch thick, using additional flour, only if necessary. Cut out the cookies and place on an ungreased baking sheet 1 inch apart. Gather the scraps into a ball, chill for at least 10 minutes, then roll out again. (If you are making round cookies without a cookie cutter, gently roll tablespoonfuls of dough into a ball with your hands.) Place the cut-out cookies on the baking sheet, leaving 1 inch between the cookies. For hand-rolled cookies, place on the baking sheet and flatten with the palm of your hand.

**5** Bake for 13 to 15 minutes in batches until the edges are pale golden. Let the cookies cool on the baking sheet for 5 minutes, then transfer to a wire rack to cool completely. The cookies can be stored in an airtight container for up to 3 days.

GRAHAM IS A TYPE of milling of whole wheat flour that was developed a century ago. The bran and germ of the grain are ground coarsely, while the endosperm is milled separately into fine white flour, and then the two are mixed together again for a coarser whole grain flour. What's interesting is that when you grind whole einkorn wheat berries, this is what happens naturally. The endosperm is soft and grinds fine like cake flour, but the bran remains coarse. I've lightened up the flavor by partially using all-purpose flour, but this recipe can also be made with all whole grain flour. MAKES 40 CRACKERS

# GOODNESS GRAHAM CRACKERS

5 tablespoons (76 g) whole milk

3 tablespoons (50 g) extra-virgin olive oil or vegetable oil

1 tablespoon honey

½ teaspoon unsulphured molasses

1½ cups (180 g) all-purpose einkorn flour

1⅓ cups (128 g) whole grain einkorn flour

¼ cup (50 g) sugar (see Note)

½ teaspoon baking powder

¼ teaspoon baking soda

⅛ teaspoon sea salt

3 tablespoons cold unsalted butter, cut into ¼-inch cubes

**1** Preheat the oven to 325°F.

**2** In a small bowl, whisk together the milk, oil, honey, and molasses until well combined.

**3** Add the flours, sugar, baking powder, baking soda, and salt to the bowl of a food processor and pulse to combine. Add the butter and pulse to distribute evenly in the dry mixture. Add the wet mixture to the food processor and process until the dough holds together in a crumbly mass.

**4** On a clean work surface, knead the dough briefly by hand until smooth. Divide the dough into 4 pieces. Transfer the first piece of dough to a silicone mat or piece of

parchment paper. Cover with parchment and use a rolling pin to roll the dough to a rough rectangle that is at least 7 × 11 inches in size and ⅛ inch thick, rolling down from the center so the dough is all the same thickness.

**5** Deeply score a ¼-inch strip along the edges of the rectangle with a sharp knife, pastry wheel, or pizza cutter to perfect the rectangular shape, but do not remove the scored strip. (As the crackers bake, the strip will brown considerably, leaving the inside crackers nice and golden.) Score the rectangle interior into crackers by pressing down to the mat or paper and cutting the rectangles in half lengthwise and then in 5 equal parts crosswise. Prick each rectangle 4 times with a fork, pressing down

until you hit the mat or paper. Transfer the crackers with the parchment or mat to a baking sheet. Repeat with a second piece of dough and spread the prepared crackers on a second baking sheet.

6 Bake the crackers for 18 minutes until golden brown and the outer edges have browned, rotating the baking sheets after 12 minutes. Slide the parchment paper or mat onto a cooling rack and cool for 5 minutes. Break the graham crackers

apart along the scored lines and let cool completely; they will crisp up when completely cooled. Proceed with rolling and baking the remaining 2 batches of crackers. The crackers can be stored for up to 1 week in an airtight container.

NOTE: These cookies are also light on sugar, so if you'd like more sweetness, mix 1 teaspoon cinnamon with 1 tablespoon of sugar to dust each batch before baking for cinnamon grahams.

**THE REASON FOR USING** melted butter instead of creamed butter in a cookie is to release the small amount of water in the butter into the flour quickly. This helps develop the flour's gluten and gives a chewier rather than crispy texture to the cookie. This technique works perfectly with einkorn flour, since the flour is slower to absorb fats, and the wonderfully soft texture of these ginger cookies is proof of that. The cookies come out of the oven really soft and although they might look underbaked, they set up perfectly after cooling. MAKES 16 LARGE COOKIES

# SOFT & CHEWY GINGER COOKIES

2½ cups (300 g) all-purpose einkorn flour

1 teaspoon baking soda

½ teaspoon fine sea salt

10 tablespoons (138 g) unsalted butter, melted and cooled slightly

½ cup (100 g) granulated sugar, plus 3 tablespoons for dusting

⅓ cup (73 g) (packed) dark brown sugar

2 tablespoons unsulphured molasses

2 teaspoons ground ginger

½ teaspoon ground cinnamon

1 large egg

1 Preheat the oven to 350°F.

2 In a medium bowl, stir together the flour, baking soda, and salt.

3 In a second bowl, stir together the butter, the ½ cup granulated sugar, the brown sugar, molasses, ginger, and cinnamon. Add the egg and whisk together until well combined. Add the flour mixture and mix with a spatula until the dry ingredients are no longer visible. Let stand for 15 minutes to give the flour time to absorb the wet ingredients.

4 Spread the remaining 3 tablespoons granulated sugar on a small plate. Roll 1½-inch (45 g) balls of dough between your hands and roll them in the sugar to dust completely.

5 Place the balls 2 inches apart on an ungreased baking sheet. Bake for 16 minutes until the cookies have spread and are barely firm to the touch. Let the cookies cool on the baking sheet for 10 minutes, then transfer to a rack to cool completely. The cookies can be stored in an airtight container for up to 3 days.

**SULTANAS, OR GOLDEN RAISINS,** pair well with golden flaxseeds and flaked whole grains of einkorn. In these cookies, I cut back on the amount of butter normally used in oatmeal cookies because einkorn does not absorb as much fat as modern wheat, and if the fat is not reduced, the cookies can spread too much. The result is a lovely, chewy cookie that feels nourishing and warm. If you do not have einkorn flakes, you may use old-fashioned oatmeal and einkorn flour, but the flavor will not be the same. MAKES 2 DOZEN COOKIES

# "OATMEAL"-FLAX SULTANAS COOKIES

1¾ cups (160 g) rolled einkorn flakes (page 20)

1 cup (140 g) sultanas, or golden raisins

3 tablespoons (20 g) golden flax meal

½ cup (118 g) boiling water

2 cups (240 g) all-purpose einkorn flour

1 teaspoon fine sea salt

¾ teaspoon baking soda

½ cup (100 g) granulated sugar

½ cup (105 g) (packed) brown sugar

1 teaspoon ground cinnamon

⅛ teaspoon ground nutmeg

12 tablespoons (160 g) unsalted butter, melted and cooled slightly

1 large egg

**1** Preheat the oven to 350°F.

**2** Mix together the einkorn flakes, sultanas, flax meal, and water with a fork in a large mixing bowl.

**3** Combine the flour, salt, and baking soda in a medium bowl.

**4** In a small bowl, mix together the sugars, cinnamon, and nutmeg. Stir in the butter and whisk until combined. Add the egg and beat with a whisk or fork until incorporated.

Stir the butter mixture into the einkorn flake mixture and mix with a spatula until just combined. Stir in the flour mixture until the dry ingredients are totally absorbed, scraping the sides and bottom of the bowl with a spatula.

**5** Drop 2-tablespoon (30 g) balls of dough 2 inches apart onto an ungreased baking sheet. Flatten each cookie slightly. Bake for 14 to 16 minutes until the cookies are browned around the edges. Transfer to a wire rack to cool completely. The cookies can be stored in an airtight container for up to 3 days.

**I FIRST HEARD ABOUT** wine cookies when my daughter Giulia tasted them at her Italian elementary school. Her classmate would bring them to school, and the kids and teacher would rave about them. Children going wild over wine cookies? I guess that only happens in Italy. Originally an ancient Roman treat, the recipe was given to me as 2 cups flour, 1 cup white wine, 1 cup sugar, and 1 cup olive oil. They can also be made with the addition of anise or fennel seeds, but I prefer them without so I can taste the delicious flavor of einkorn. These cookies store very well and are a nice choice for those who avoid eating dairy and eggs. MAKES ABOUT 24 COOKIES

# OLIVE OIL & WINE COOKIES

½ cup (100 g) sugar

2 cups plus 2 tablespoons (270 g) all-purpose einkorn flour

Pinch of baking powder

½ teaspoon fine sea salt

6 tablespoons (75 g) extra-virgin olive oil, plus 1 teaspoon for brushing

6 tablespoons (80 g) dry white wine

**1** Set aside 1 tablespoon of the sugar on a small plate.

**2** In a medium bowl, combine the remaining 7 tablespoons (87 g) sugar, flour, baking powder, and salt. Drizzle the oil over the flour and mix with a fork until the dough is very clumpy. Add the wine and continue mixing with the fork. The dough will seem overly wet, but keep working until the flour has absorbed the liquid. Knead the dough on a clean work surface for about 2 minutes until smooth. Cover the bowl with plastic wrap and refrigerate for 30 minutes.

**3** Preheat the oven to 350°F. Line a baking sheet with parchment paper.

**4** Take 1 tablespoon of the dough and roll it between the palms of your hands to form a ball. Place the ball of dough on your work surface and roll with your fingers until it is about 5 inches long. Form a circle by pressing together the 2 ends. Brush the cookie with olive oil and dip the top of the cookie into the reserved sugar to dust lightly. Place the cookies on the baking sheet, spacing them 1½ inches apart. Continue in the same manner until you have formed all of the cookies.

**5** Bake for 25 minutes until the edges have begun to brown. Remove the cookies from the baking sheet and transfer to a cooling rack. Let cool completely before serving. The cookies can be stored in an airtight container for up to 7 days.

CHOCOLATE CHIP COOKIES BAKED with einkorn are exceptionally delicious yet can be difficult to get just right—and that may be true for all chocolate chip cookies. For me, the perfect chocolate chip cookie has a balance between a bit of crispiness around the edges and a soft and chewy center. To get this just right, bake in batches and store the dough in the refrigerator between each batch. Line a baking sheet with parchment paper or a silicone baking mat to avoid sticking. Clean the baking sheet with cold water between batches to bring it back to room temperature. (Otherwise the warm baking sheet will cause the cookies to spread.) MAKES ABOUT 24 COOKIES

# CHOCOLATE CHIP COOKIES

2 cups (240 g) all-purpose einkorn flour

1/2 teaspoon baking soda

1 teaspoon fine sea salt

10 tablespoons (138 g) unsalted butter

3/4 cup (150 g) granulated sugar

1/2 cup (110 g) (packed) dark brown sugar

2 large eggs, one separated

1/4 teaspoon pure vanilla extract

1 1/4 cups (210 g) semisweet chocolate chips

**1** Preheat the oven to 375°F. Line a baking sheet with parchment paper or a silicone mat.

**2** In a medium bowl, stir together the flour, baking soda, and salt. Set aside.

**3** In the bowl of a standing mixer fitted with a paddle attachment, cream together the butter and sugars for 2 minutes, stopping a few times to scrape down the sides. Add 1 egg, the separated egg yolk, and vanilla and beat on medium-low speed for 1 to 2 minutes until thoroughly combined. Add the flour mixture and beat on medium-low speed just until the flour is incorporated.

Add the chocolate chips and continue beating until the dough is evenly mixed. Do not overmix, or the dough will get too warm. Refrigerate for 15 minutes.

**4** Roll 2-tablespoon (35 g) scoops of cookie dough in your hands into balls and place on the prepared baking sheet, leaving 2 inches around each cookie. Bake the cookies in batches for 14 minutes until the edges are golden and the center is soft but cooked through. Let the cookies cool on the baking sheet for 5 minutes. Transfer to a cooling rack. The cookies can be stored in an airtight container for up to 3 days.

IN ITALY, *pan di Spagna*, or Spanish bread, is a light, spongy cake that is made without added fat, which makes it well suited to einkorn flour. The basic recipe can be used as the base for a variety of cream-filled cakes such as *zuppa inglese*, and you can also enjoy it simply topped with powdered sugar or frosted with mascarpone cream, as it is here. The mascarpone serves to stabilize the whipped cream, making it thick enough for spreading, not to mention very delicious and much less sweet than buttercream frosting. MAKES ONE 9-INCH CAKE

# SPONGE CAKE WITH STRAWBERRIES & MASCARPONE CREAM

FOR THE STRAWBERRIES

6 cups (2 pounds) fresh strawberries, hulled and sliced

¼ cup (50 g) granulated sugar

FOR THE SPONGE CAKE

Vegetable oil, for greasing the pan

1 cup (120 g) all-purpose einkorn flour, plus more for dusting

5 large eggs, at room temperature and separated

¾ cup (150 g) granulated sugar

½ teaspoon fine sea salt

Finely grated zest from ½ lemon

FOR THE MASCARPONE WHIPPED CREAM FROSTING

1 cup (228 g) mascarpone cheese

1 cup (240 g) heavy cream

2 tablespoons powdered sugar

1 **PREPARE THE STRAWBERRIES:** In a large bowl, mix together the strawberries and granulated sugar. Place in the refrigerator and let the strawberries macerate for 30 to 45 minutes.

2 **MAKE THE CAKE:** Preheat the oven to 350°F. Lightly grease the bottom and sides of a 9-inch round cake pan. Place a round piece of parchment paper on the bottom.

Brush the paper lightly with oil and lightly dust the bottom and sides with flour. Tap out the excess flour.

3 In a standing mixer fitted with a wire whip attachment, add the egg yolks, ½ cup (100 g) of the sugar, salt, and lemon zest and process on medium-high speed for 3 minutes until thick and pale yellow. Pour the mixture into a large bowl.

(continues)

**4** Clean and dry the mixer bowl. Add the egg whites to the bowl and beat on medium speed for 1 to 2 minutes until the whites hold soft peaks. With the mixer running, slowly add the remaining ¼ cup (50 g) sugar and beat for 1 minute until stiff and glossy.

**5** Fold a third of the whites into the yolk mixture. Sift the flour into a small bowl, then sift and fold half of the flour into the yolk mixture. Fold in another one third of the whites, then the rest of the flour, and finish off with the whites.

**6** Pour the batter into the cake pan. Bake for 35 to 37 minutes until the center of the cake springs back when you press on it. Do not open the oven to test doneness or to rotate the pan until the center of the cake has risen fully. The cake will rise to a high dome and then deflate when out of the oven. Let the cake cool in the pan for 10 minutes, then turn out onto a rack to cool completely before assembling.

**7** MAKE THE FROSTING: Add the mascarpone, cream, and powdered sugar to a bowl of the standing mixer fitted with a wire whip attachment. Beat on low speed for 30 seconds to combine. Increase the speed to medium and whip for 3 minutes until the mixture holds peaks. Don't overbeat or the frosting will look grainy, and don't raise the speed higher than medium, even if the mixture is not thickening at 2 minutes. (You can make the frosting 1 hour ahead, wrap tightly, and refrigerate.)

**8** To assemble, slice the cake in half horizontally with a long serrated knife to form 2 thin layers. Place 1 layer on a 10-inch cake dish and tuck small strips of parchment paper around the edges of the cake to keep the dish clean while you frost the cake. Spread ¾ cup of the frosting evenly over the layer. Add all of the strawberries and juices on top. Place the top layer over the strawberries and press down gently. Spread ¾ cup of the frosting on the sides of the cake. Spread the remaining frosting around the top of the cake, forming twirls and peaks. Remove the paper. This cake is best served immediately. However, you can make the cake up to 3 hours ahead and refrigerate it.

**THIS SATISFYING CARROT CAKE** is lighter on sugar than usual owing to the natural sweetness you get from puréeing half of the carrots and the raisins to add to the batter. In Italy, almonds are often paired with carrots, but if you like walnuts or want to make this a nut-free cake, feel free to adjust to your tastes. It almost seems a shame to frost such a wholesome cake, but if you please, nothing's better than cream cheese frosting. To make a double layer cake, bake two 9-inch cakes and double the frosting recipe. MAKES ONE 9-INCH CAKE

# CLASSIC CARROT CAKE

FOR THE CARROT CAKE

¾ cup (150 g) extra-virgin olive oil, plus more for greasing the pan

1½ cups (180 g) all-purpose einkorn flour, plus more for dusting

1 teaspoon baking powder

½ teaspoon baking soda

½ teaspoon fine sea salt

½ teaspoon ground cinnamon

¼ teaspoon ground ginger

½ cup (80 g) raisins

2 cups (256 g) (packed) grated carrots (from 3 to 4 large carrots)

2 large eggs

¾ cup (155 g) (packed) dark brown sugar

½ cup (60 g) slivered almonds

FOR THE CREAM CHEESE FROSTING

8 ounces (225 g) cream cheese, at room temperature

6 tablespoons (90 g) unsalted butter, at room temperature

1 cup (120 g) powdered sugar

**1** MAKE THE CAKE: Preheat the oven to 350°F. Grease and flour a round or square 9-inch cake pan and line the bottom with a piece of parchment paper cut to the size of the pan, then grease and flour the parchment.

**2** In a medium bowl, sift together the einkorn flour, baking powder, baking soda, salt, cinnamon, and ginger.

**3** In a blender, combine the oil, raisins, and 1 cup of the carrots. Purée for 1 minute until the carrots and raisins are finely chopped.

**4** In the bowl of a standing mixer, add the eggs and beat on medium speed for

1 minute. Add the brown sugar and increase the speed to high and beat for 3 minutes until light and fluffy. Using a spatula, fold half of the flour mixture into the sugar mixture and when it is almost completely absorbed, fold in half of the oil mixture. Repeat. Fold in the remaining 1 cup carrots in 2 batches. Fold in the almonds, then pour the batter into the cake pan.

**5** Bake the cake for 55 to 60 minutes until the tip of a toothpick inserted in the center comes out entirely dry and the cake has started to pull away from the sides of the pan. Place the pan on a rack to cool for 30 minutes, then invert the cake on a rack and allow it to cool completely before frosting.

**6** **MAKE THE FROSTING:** Add the cream cheese to the bowl of a standing mixer fitted with a paddle attachment. Beat on medium speed for 2 minutes. Add the butter and beat for 1 to 2 minutes until smooth and creamy. Sift the sugar and add it to the bowl. Beat for 1 minute more. You can cover the frosting tightly and refrigerate it for up to 2 days ahead. Let soften to room temperature before using.

**7** To assemble, place the cake on a 10-inch cake dish. Spread ¾ to 1 cup of the frosting on top of the cake. Spread the remaining frosting on the sides of the cake and serve immediately. The cake can be stored in the refrigerator for up to 3 days and served chilled.

**MADE WITH FOUR DIFFERENT** coconut-derived products—oil, flour, flakes, and milk—the rich flavor of this dairy-free pound cake will bring you back for a second slice. I've made a few tweaks to the mixing technique and proportions used in a classic pound cake to give it a better spring in the oven. The batter might seem thick, but the cake will bake up very moist. MAKES 1 POUND CAKE

# DAIRY-FREE COCONUT POUND CAKE

FOR THE CAKE

½ cup (100 g) extra-virgin coconut oil, melted and cooled slightly, plus more for greasing the pan

2 cups (240 g) all-purpose einkorn flour, plus more for dusting

¼ cup (30 g) coconut flour

1 tablespoon baking powder

½ teaspoon fine sea salt

¼ cup (20 g) unsweetened flaked coconut

3 large eggs

¾ cup (150 g) granulated sugar

½ cup (120 g) coconut milk

FOR THE GLAZE

¾ cup (90 g) powdered sugar

2 tablespoons coconut milk

1 tablespoon unsweetened flaked coconut

**1** MAKE THE CAKE: Preheat the oven to 350°F. Grease and flour an 8½ × 4½-inch loaf pan.

**2** In a medium bowl, sift together the flours, baking powder, and salt. Stir in the flaked coconut.

**3** In the bowl of a standing mixer fitted with a paddle attachment, add the eggs and process on medium speed for 1 minute to break up the yolks. Add the granulated sugar and mix on high for 3 minutes until thick and creamy. Remove the bowl from the mixer and whisk in one third of the flour mixture. Whisk in ¼ cup of the coconut milk. Continue in this manner until you have

finished adding the flour and the milk. Fold in the ½ cup oil until incorporated and smooth.

**4** Pour the batter into the pan. Bake for 1 hour until a toothpick inserted in the center comes out clean. Cool the cake in the pan on a rack for 10 minutes. Invert the cake and place on a rack to cool completely before glazing.

**5** MAKE THE GLAZE: Whisk together the powdered sugar and coconut milk to form a pourable glaze. Stir in the flaked coconut. Set the cake and rack on top of a piece of parchment paper. Drizzle the cake with the glaze and let set for 1 hour before serving. The cake can be stored in an airtight container for up to 5 days.

**SURE TO BE A** hit at birthday celebrations, these cupcakes are very easy to make. Children love the lovely yellow cupcakes as well as the frosting, which has a vibrant pink color and tang from freeze-dried strawberries. The buttery flavor of einkorn will make these cupcakes some of the best your guests have ever tasted. If these einkorn cupcakes are for a special occasion, I would recommend procuring a vanilla bean pod for the ultimate touch of flavor. Be sure to sift the flour twice so that it is completely absorbed and doesn't clump up during folding. The strawberries may also be omitted for a simple cream cheese frosting. MAKES 12 CUPCAKES

# VANILLA CUPCAKES WITH STRAWBERRY CREAM CHEESE FROSTING

FOR THE VANILLA
CUPCAKES

1 cup (120 g) all-purpose
einkorn flour

1 teaspoon baking powder

¼ teaspoon fine sea salt

6 tablespoons (90 g) unsalted
butter, melted

¼ cup (60 g) plain yogurt

Seeds from ½ vanilla bean,
or ½ teaspoon pure vanilla
extract

2 large eggs

⅔ cup (135 g) granulated sugar

FOR THE STRAWBERRY
CREAM CHEESE FROSTING

½ cup (15 g) freeze-dried
strawberries

4 ounces (115 g) cream
cheese, at room temperature

4 tablespoons (56 g)
unsalted butter, at room
temperature

1½ cups (180 g) powdered
sugar

Pinch of salt

Fresh strawberry slices,
for garnishing

**1** MAKE THE CUPCAKES: Preheat the oven to 350°F. Fill a muffin tin with 12 paper liners.

**2** In a medium bowl, sift together the flour, baking powder, and salt.

**3** In a small bowl, stir together the butter, yogurt, and vanilla seeds.

**4** In the bowl of a standing mixer fitted with a paddle attachment, beat the eggs on medium speed for 30 seconds. Add the granulated sugar, increase the speed to high, and beat for 1 minute until the egg mixture begins to thicken. Detach the bowl from the mixer and sift in half of the flour mixture, folding in with a spatula. When it is almost completely absorbed, fold in half of the butter mixture. Repeat with the remaining flour and butter mixtures until completely used.

**5** Fill the muffin cups to halfway full with the batter. Bake for 20 minutes until the cupcakes are lightly golden on top and a toothpick inserted into the center comes out clean. Transfer the pan to a wire rack and let cool for 5 minutes. Remove the cupcakes from the pan and cool on a rack until completely cooled, about 1 hour.

**6** MAKE THE FROSTING: Grind the dried strawberries in a blender or food processor until you have a fine powder.

**7** Add the cream cheese to the bowl of a standing mixer fitted with a paddle attachment. Beat on medium-high speed

for 2 minutes. Add the butter and beat for 1 to 2 minutes until smooth and creamy. Scrape down the sides and bottom of the bowl. Sift in the powdered sugar and salt and beat briefly to combine, then add the strawberry powder. Beat for 30 seconds more. The frosting can be stored, covered tightly and refrigerated, for up to 1 day. Let soften at room temperature before using.

**8** To serve, spread the frosting on the cupcakes and garnish with the strawberry slices. The cupcakes can be stored in an airtight container at room temperature for up to 1 day and in the refrigerator for 3 days.

**THESE CHOCOLATE CUPCAKES, TOPPED** with chocolate frosting, bake up perfectly for a special occasion. Opting for cocoa powder instead of bakers' chocolate and using less butter in this batter is what makes them perfect with einkorn. I like to pipe the chocolate buttercream frosting on the cupcakes and then sprinkle chocolate chips on top. MAKES 12 CUPCAKES

# CHOCOLATE CUPCAKES
## WITH CHOCOLATE CHIP BUTTERCREAM FROSTING

FOR THE CUPCAKES

¾ cup (90 g) all-purpose einkorn flour

1 teaspoon baking powder

½ teaspoon fine sea salt

5 tablespoons (70 g) unsalted butter, melted

¼ cup (24 g) cocoa powder

⅓ cup (80 g) buttermilk

2 large eggs

¾ cup (150 g) granulated sugar

FOR THE CHOCOLATE CHIP BUTTERCREAM FROSTING

12 tablespoons (170 g) unsalted butter, at room temperature

1¼ cups (150 g) powdered sugar

2 tablespoons cocoa powder

Pinch of salt

¼ cup (42 g) bittersweet chocolate chips, for sprinkling

**1** MAKE THE CUPCAKES: Preheat the oven to 350°F. Fill a muffin tin with 12 paper liners.

**2** Sift together the flour, baking powder, and salt into a medium bowl.

**3** In a small bowl, whisk together the butter and cocoa powder until smooth. Whisk in the buttermilk.

**4** In the bowl of a standing mixer fitted with a paddle attachment, beat the eggs on medium speed for 30 seconds. Add the granulated sugar and beat on high for 2 minutes until the mixture begins to thicken. Detach the bowl from the mixer and sift half of the flour mixture into the bowl. Using a spatula, fold in until almost completely absorbed. Fold in half of the cocoa mixture until the batter is smooth. Repeat with the remaining flour and cocoa mixtures.

**5** Fill the muffin cups two thirds with batter. Bake for 20 to 22 minutes until a toothpick inserted into the center of a cupcake comes out clean. Transfer the pan to a wire rack and let cool for 10 minutes. Remove the cupcakes from the pan and set on a rack until completely cooled, about 1 hour.

**6** MAKE THE FROSTING: Cream the butter in a standing mixer fitted with a paddle attachment on medium speed for 3 minutes until fluffy. Sift the sugar, cocoa powder, and salt into the bowl and process on low for 30 seconds. The frosting can be stored, covered tightly and refrigerated, for up to 2 days. Let soften at room temperature before using.

**7** Fill a pastry bag fitted with a large open star tip. Pipe the frosting on the cupcakes, then sprinkle the chocolate chips on top. The cupcakes can be stored in an airtight container at room temperature for up to 1 day and in the refrigerator for 3 days.

**WITH NO ADDED SPICES** or chocolate to get in the way, this completely whole grain cake touts the remarkable flavor of einkorn in every bite. Baking cakes with whole grain einkorn can be very tricky because the flour absorbs water very slowly, so you often end up with a very dry crumb. The solution is to let the batter rest in the refrigerator for 1 hour before baking, so the flour hydrates completely before going into the oven. Moist, wholesome, and absolutely delicious, especially with the delectable caramel glaze made from dark brown sugar, this is a cake you will come back to again and again. MAKES 1 CAKE

# WHOLE GRAIN BUNDT CAKE WITH RUM CARAMEL GLAZE

### FOR THE CAKE

4 cups (384 g) whole grain einkorn flour, plus more for dusting

1 tablespoon baking powder

½ teaspoon baking soda

½ teaspoon fine sea salt

8 tablespoons (113 g) unsalted butter, at room temperature, plus more for greasing the pan

½ cup (100 g) granulated sugar

½ cup (105 g) (packed) dark brown sugar

3 large eggs

1½ cups (344 g) kefir

### FOR THE RUM CARAMEL GLAZE

4 tablespoons (55 g) unsalted butter

1 tablespoon light rum

¼ cup (55 g) (packed) dark brown sugar

Pinch of salt

**1** MAKE THE CAKE: In a large bowl, mix together the flour, baking powder, baking soda, and salt.

**2** In the bowl of a standing mixer fitted with a paddle attachment, beat the butter on medium speed for 1 minute until smooth and creamy, scraping the sides and bottom of the bowl. Add the sugars, increase the speed to medium-high, and beat for 2 minutes until light and fluffy. Add the eggs, one at a time, mixing on medium for 30 seconds after each addition to incorporate fully. Fold in the kefir with a spatula. Fold the flour mixture into the wet

mixture, mixing until fully incorporated. Cover the bowl with plastic wrap and refrigerate for 1 hour.

**3** Preheat the oven to 350°F. Butter and flour a 10- or 12-cup fluted Bundt pan. Pour the batter into the prepared pan. Bake for 45 to 50 minutes until a skewer inserted in the middle of the cake comes out clean. Place the pan on a rack to cool for 15 minutes. Loosen the edges of the cake from the pan with a sharp knife. Invert the pan onto a serving dish. If the cake does not dislodge from the pan, grasp the plate with your fingers underneath and your thumbs on the pan. Give the pan a

good shake to loosen. Invert the cake onto a cooling rack and cool completely before glazing.

4  **MAKE THE GLAZE:** Melt the butter in a medium skillet over low heat. Increase the heat to medium-low, add the rum, and simmer for 1 minute. Whisk in the brown sugar, 1 tablespoon of water, and salt. Once the mixture begins to bubble, reduce the heat to low and simmer for 3 to 4 minutes until the caramel has thickened, stirring

constantly. Transfer to a small bowl and let cool for 5 minutes, stirring occasionally, until the glaze is pourable but thick enough to adhere to the cake.

5  Place the cake on a rack over a piece of parchment paper. Drizzle the glaze over the cake. Transfer to a serving platter and serve immediately. The cake can be stored in an airtight container for up to 3 days.

**EVEN THOUGH BROWNIES CONTAIN** very little flour, making them with einkorn can be a bit tricky. When mixed into very thick and rich batters, einkorn flour causes the crumb to become gummy, not moist and rich. I work around that by beating the eggs until creamy before folding in the chocolate and flour. Everyone has a personal preference for brownies, and this recipe can be easily adjusted to suit your taste. I love dark chocolate, but if you prefer a less intense chocolate flavor, you can substitute semisweet chocolate with 65% cocoa for the bittersweet chocolate.

MAKES 16 TWO-INCH BROWNIES

# FUDGY DARK CHOCOLATE BROWNIES

6 tablespoons (83 g) cold unsalted butter, cut into ¼-inch cubes, plus more for greasing the pan

5 ounces (142 g) bittersweet chocolate (70%), chopped

2 tablespoons unsweetened cocoa powder

3 large eggs

1 cup (200 g) sugar

¼ teaspoon fine sea salt

¾ cup (90 g) all-purpose einkorn flour

**1** Preheat the oven to 325°F. Butter an 8-inch square pan. Cut a piece of parchment paper 7 inches wide and place in the pan, creasing at the bottom of the pan and allowing the rest to hang over the edges.

**2** Place the butter and chocolate in a medium heatproof bowl. Place over a saucepan of simmering water without letting the bowl touch the water. Stir frequently until the mixture is melted. Remove the bowl from the heat and stir in the cocoa powder until smooth. Set aside.

**3** In the bowl of a standing mixer fitted with a paddle attachment, beat the eggs on medium speed for 1 minute. Add the sugar and salt. Beat on high for 2 minutes until creamy and light yellow. Fold in one third of the chocolate mixture with a spatula by

hand. Sift in half of the flour, then fold from the bottom of the bowl to incorporate the chocolate. When the flour is mostly absorbed, proceed in the same manner with the remaining mixture.

**4** Pour the batter into the center of the pan. Do not shake or tilt the pan; the batter will spread evenly in the oven, and this will give you that light shiny surface typical of a great brownie.

**5** Bake for 33 to 35 minutes until a toothpick inserted in the center comes out with a bit of moist crumbs attached.

**6** Cool in the pan on a wire rack for 30 minutes. Use the parchment to lift the brownies; let cool completely before slicing and serving. Store in an airtight container at room temperature for up to 3 days.

**UNLIKE OTHER CHOCOLATE LAYER** cakes, the Brooklyn Blackout Cake is frosted with a chocolate pudding instead of buttercream frosting, which adds a light moistness to a rich cake. The original recipe was lost when the Brooklyn bakery that created it in the World War II era closed its doors. I have taken some liberties by using 2 instead of 3 layers and by adding a stiff chocolate buttercream as the filling. My version of this luscious chocolate cake is not overly sweet, and the basic chocolate cake can be frosted any way you like. MAKES ONE 9-INCH CAKE

# BROOKLYN BLACKOUT CAKE

### FOR THE CHOCOLATE LAYER CAKE

8 tablespoons (113 g) unsalted butter, at room temperature, plus more for greasing the pan

½ cup (60 g) cocoa powder, plus more for dusting

1¼ cups (150 g) all-purpose einkorn flour

2 teaspoons baking powder

½ teaspoon baking soda

½ teaspoon fine sea salt

1 cup (244 g) hot whole milk

2 ounces (56 g) bittersweet chocolate (70%), chopped

¼ cup (50 g) extra-virgin olive oil or vegetable oil

1 cup (200 g) granulated sugar

4 large eggs

### FOR THE CHOCOLATE BUTTERCREAM FILLING

2 ounces (56 g) bittersweet chocolate (70%), chopped

4 tablespoons (56 g) unsalted butter, at room temperature

½ cup (62 g) powdered sugar

### FOR THE CHOCOLATE PUDDING FROSTING

½ cup (100 g) granulated sugar

¼ cup (30 g) cocoa powder

⅓ cup (40 g) cornstarch

⅛ teaspoon fine sea salt

1½ cups (365 g) whole milk

2 large eggs

**1** MAKE THE CAKE: Preheat the oven to 350°F. Butter a 9-inch round cake pan. Line the bottom with a piece of parchment paper cut to the size of the pan. Dust the sides of the pan with cocoa powder.

**2** Sift together the flour, baking powder, baking soda, and salt into a medium bowl.

**3** In another medium bowl, whisk together the milk and chocolate until the chocolate has melted. Whisk in the cocoa powder and mix until the mixture is smooth. Whisk in the oil until the mixture emulsifies.

**4** In the bowl of a standing mixer fitted with a paddle attachment, beat the butter on medium for 1 minute until smooth and creamy, scraping the sides and bottom of the bowl. Add the granulated sugar, increase the speed to medium-high, and beat for 3 to 4 minutes until light and fluffy. Add the eggs, one at a time, mixing on medium for 30 seconds after each addition to incorporate fully. Reduce the

(continues)

speed to medium-low. Add the chocolate mixture and beat until combined. Sift half of the flour mixture on top of the bowl and fold in with a spatula until the flour is almost completely absorbed. Repeat with the remaining flour, folding until the batter has absorbed all of the flour.

5 Pour the batter into the prepared pan. Bake for 50 to 55 minutes until the cake springs back when pressed in the center. Let cool in the pan on a wire rack for 30 minutes. Invert the cake onto the rack, lift off the pan, and slowly peel off the parchment paper. Let the cake cool completely for 30 minutes more.

6 MAKE THE FILLING: Melt the chocolate in the top of a double boiler over barely simmering water. Stir often until completely melted. Remove the bowl from the heat and let cool for 10 minutes.

7 In the bowl of a standing mixer fitted with a paddle attachment, cream the butter on medium speed for 1 minute until light and fluffy. Reduce the speed to low. Add the powdered sugar and beat for 30 seconds to 1 minute to combine. Pour in the melted chocolate. Increase the speed to medium and beat for 2 minutes until smooth and fluffy.

8 MAKE THE FROSTING: Whisk together the granulated sugar, cocoa, cornstarch, and salt in a medium bowl.

9 In a medium saucepan, whisk together the milk and eggs. Bring to a simmer on low heat, whisking constantly, for about 5 minutes. Whisk the milk mixture into the dry ingredients until well incorporated. Pour the mixture back into the saucepan through a sieve to remove any lumps. Press the sieve with the back of a spoon and scrape the bottom to ensure all of the mixture is added to the pan.

10 Simmer the pudding on low heat, whisking continuously until thickened, 6 to 10 minutes. The mixture will seem very thin for most of the cooking time and then begin to thicken rapidly. Once the mixture starts to thicken, continue to cook on low for 2 minutes. You may be tempted to increase the heat if you do not see the pudding thickening, but leave it as is, or the eggs will curdle and the mixture will become clumpy. Pour the thickened pudding into a clean bowl and let cool for 10 minutes, stirring frequently, before frosting the cake.

11 To assemble, slice the cake in half horizontally with a long serrated knife. Place the bottom layer on a rack over a baking tray. Spread the buttercream filling evenly over the bottom layer with an offset spatula. Place the second layer on top. Spoon half of the pudding frosting on top, then add more frosting around the sides of the cake. Smooth out the frosting with the spatula. Use the back of the spoon to make swirls on the top and along the sides of the cake.

12 Serve at room temperature. The cake can be stored in an airtight container in the refrigerator for up to 3 days.

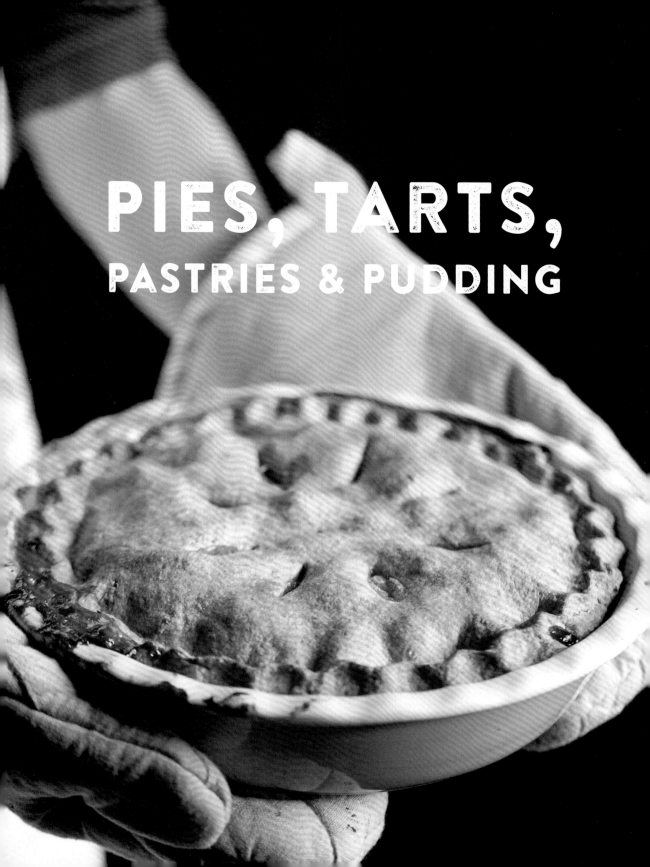

# PIES, TARTS,
## PASTRIES & PUDDING

Classic Apple Pie, page 146

THIS CHAPTER WILL PROVIDE YOU WITH A NICE COLLECTION of pie and tart crust recipes. When made with einkorn flour, Classic Apple Pie (page 146) is exceptionally flavorful as well as beautifully golden in color. The semi–whole grain free-form Blueberry Galette (page 150), which you can bake with all seasonal fruits, is gorgeous straight out of the oven. The eggs in the crust for Sour Cherry Crostata (page 149) help to make the dough more pliable, easier for creating its simple lattice top. Apricot Custard Tartlets (page 153) incorporate melted butter into the flour, which lends crispiness to the crust that contrasts well with the custard and soft apricot topping. I had a lot of fun creating my favorite Italian pastry with einkorn, Italian Cream Puffs (page 162), which will generate lots of smiles when you serve them to friends and family at the close of a special meal.

Substituting white rice with einkorn wheat berries in the Spiced Wheat Berry Custard Tart (page 158) and Einkorn "Rice" Pudding (page 165) delivers a wholesome goodness that is very unique. When I first served the custard tart to guests at my cooking classes in Lucca, they could not stop raving over how delicious the flavor was. I was not sure how they would like the texture of chewy wheat berries baked inside a tart, but I think the addition of bay leaves and a clove really gives the filling a lovely flavor.

As you are learning, you'll find that einkorn dough is not as elastic as dough made with modern wheat, so you will have more tearing than normal when rolling out the pie and tart crusts. Refrigerating the dough will help immensely; just refrain from adding additional flour. Actually, when you first start adding water after cutting in the butter, the dough will seem rather dry as the fats are absorbed, but the dough will quickly turn from dry to wet as you knead and then bake up perfectly flavorful in all of these recipes.

**HERE IS A BASIC** sweet dough recipe that I like to roll into these irresistible sticky cinnamon buns, which I guarantee will disappear fast once they hit the breakfast table. I recommend using soured milk like buttermilk or yogurt, but if you are intolerant to dairy, you may substitute water. I like to mix the melted butter with the sugar before spreading because the dough seems to absorb it better. Some sugar and butter will leak out during baking and form a delicious caramel on the bottom of the bun which will become the top of the bun inverted. I also love to sprinkle currants on top of the cinnamon sugar before baking for a touch of added flavor. A nice alternative to the cinnamon sugar and butter filling is raspberry jam and goat cheese. Instead of cutting into buns, try shaping the cylinder of dough into a lovely Swedish tea ring. MAKES 10 CINNAMON BUNS

# SLOW-RISE STICKY CINNAMON BUNS

### FOR THE DOUGH

¼ cup (60 g) refreshed Einkorn Sourdough Starter (page 13), or 1 teaspoon active dry yeast

1 cup (245 g) buttermilk or plain yogurt

2 large eggs

½ cup (100 g) granulated sugar

1 tablespoon ground cinnamon

5 cups (600 g) all-purpose einkorn flour, plus more for dusting

1 teaspoon fine sea salt

2 tablespoons (30 g) unsalted butter, melted and cooled

### FOR THE FILLING

½ cup (105 g) (packed) dark brown sugar

1 tablespoon all-purpose einkorn flour

2 teaspoons ground cinnamon

⅛ teaspoon fine sea salt

6 tablespoons (83 g) unsalted butter, melted

3 tablespoons dried currants

### FOR THE GLAZE

½ cup (60 g) powdered sugar

2½ teaspoons warm water

(continues)

**1** MAKE THE DOUGH: In a large bowl, mix the starter or yeast with buttermilk or yogurt, eggs, granulated sugar, and cinnamon. Add the flour, sprinkle the salt on top, and mix with a spatula as much as you can. Add the butter and knead the dough by hand in the bowl until the dough starts to hold together. Transfer the dough to a work surface and knead until smooth. Place the dough back in the bowl and cover with plastic wrap. Let rest for 15 minutes.

**2** Turn the dough (see page 15) one time. Transfer to the bowl and cover the dough tightly with plastic wrap. If you are using sourdough, let the dough proof at room temperature for 8 to 10 hours until the dough has risen by roughly one third. If you are using yeast, place the dough in the refrigerator for 8 to 10 hours.

**3** Lightly dust a 24-inch-long piece of parchment paper with flour. Transfer the dough to the paper and roll the dough to a 12 × 18-inch rectangle.

**4** MAKE THE FILLING: In a small bowl, mix together the brown sugar, flour, cinnamon, and salt. Mix in the butter. Spread the mixture over the rectangle of dough reaching all the way to the sides, leaving a 3-inch border along one long side. Sprinkle the currants on top. Roll the dough across its width to form a long, fairly tight cylinder. When you get to the plain strip of dough at the end, pull up the dough and press to seal.

**5** Line a baking sheet with parchment paper. Cut the dough into 2-inch-thick rounds and place cut side down on the baking sheet, spacing them 2 inches apart. (Alternatively, you can place the buns in 2 buttered 9-inch cake pans.) Cover with plastic wrap and let rest for 1 hour. Preheat the oven to 375°F.

**6** Bake the rolls for 28 minutes until evenly golden and firm. Let cool for 10 minutes on the baking sheet or cake pans. Lift with a metal spatula or invert the cake pans onto a wire rack to cool for 15 minutes before glazing.

**7** MAKE THE GLAZE: Combine the powdered sugar and water in a small bowl. Drizzle the glaze in strips over the buns. Serve warm. The buns can be stored, tightly wrapped, at room temperature for up to 3 days.

THIS PIE IS MADE with a short-crust pastry dough, also known as *pâte brisée*, which is suited for baking fresh fruit pies as well as tarts and savory quiches. Break up the cold butter into very fine pieces so that more of it touches the flour, and you will have a flaky and delicate crust. I prefer to cook down the apples briefly before filling the pie, which allows me to really fill the pie with fruit and prevents a gap from forming between the top crust and the fruit during baking. Tart Granny Smith apples are a great choice for this pie. Chilling the bottom crust keeps it from becoming soggy during baking. MAKES ONE 9-INCH PIE

# CLASSIC APPLE PIE

FOR THE APPLE FILLING

2 tablespoons unsalted butter

2¾ pounds (1.25 kg) large tart apples (about 8), peeled, cored, and cut into ¼-inch-thick slices

¾ cup (150 g) sugar

3 tablespoons all-purpose einkorn flour

1 teaspoon ground cinnamon

¼ teaspoon ground nutmeg

½ teaspoon fine sea salt

2 tablespoons fresh lemon juice

FOR THE PIE DOUGH

2½ cups (300 g) all-purpose einkorn flour, plus more for dusting

¾ teaspoon fine sea salt

12 tablespoons (166 g) cold unsalted butter, cut into ¼-inch cubes

¼ cup (59 g) ice water

1 teaspoon whole milk, for brushing

**1** MAKE THE FILLING: Melt the butter on low heat in a large saucepan, add the apples, and toss with the butter until coated. Increase the heat to medium-low, cover the pan, and cook for 8 minutes until the apples have softened, stirring occasionally.

**2** In a small bowl, combine the sugar, flour, cinnamon, nutmeg, and salt.

**3** Once the fruit is cooked, transfer to a large bowl and mix in the lemon juice, then toss in the sugar mixture until the apples are evenly coated. Let cool while you prepare the dough.

**4** Preheat the oven to 425°F.

**5** MAKE THE PIE DOUGH: Combine the flour and salt in a large bowl. Cut in the butter with a pastry blender until the mixture is sandy and you can't get the chunks of butter any finer. Add the water and mix in just to combine, then gently knead with your hands in the bowl until the dough just holds together when pressed into a ball. Divide the dough in half. Form each half into a disc, and wrap one half in plastic wrap and refrigerate for 20 minutes.

**6** Place the unwrapped dough half on lightly floured parchment paper. Dust the top of the dough and your rolling pin lightly with flour, and roll the dough out to 1 inch larger than the rim of your pie dish and about ⅛ inch thick, lifting and turning the dough with each roll. (If your rolling pin sticks to the dough, dust the pin with flour each time.) Invert the dough into the pie dish, remove the paper, and gently press into the bottom edges and up the sides, with some dough overhanging the edges. Refrigerate the pie dish for 20 minutes.

**7** Remove the remaining dough half from the refrigerator and roll out the top crust in the same manner as the bottom.

**8** Remove the chilled pie dish from the refrigerator. Pour the apples into the pie dish. Top with the other piece of dough and press the edges to seal. Fold and tuck under the overhanging dough toward the rim of the dish. Crimp the edges of the pie with your fingers, and brush the top of the pie with the milk. Cut six 2-inch-long vents in the top of the pie.

**9** Place the pie on top of a baking sheet to catch drippings. Bake for 20 minutes until the top of the crust starts to brown. Reduce the oven temperature to 375°F and bake for 40 minutes more until the crust is deeply golden brown on top. Serve warm or at room temperature. The pie may be stored in an airtight container in the refrigerator for 3 days.

IN ITALY, TARTS ARE generally made with jam rather than fresh fruit. When my daughters started elementary school, we discovered that sour cherry crostata was the go-to sweet to bring for birthday parties. The marmalade bakes firm and the pie's crust is rather compact, so it is easy to eat with your hands without much of a mess. Italians slice the finished crostata into small squares and prefer a tart fruit filling, such as sour cherry, plum, or apricot, so that the tang of the marmalade balances the lightly sweetened crust. MAKES ONE 9½-INCH TART

# SOUR CHERRY CROSTATA

2 cups (240 g) all-purpose einkorn flour, plus more for dusting

¼ teaspoon baking powder

¼ teaspoon fine sea salt

2 large eggs, one separated

8 tablespoons (113 g) unsalted butter, at room temperature

¼ cup (50 g) sugar

Zest of ½ lemon

1 cup (280 g) sour cherry preserves

**1** On a clean work surface, mix the flour with the baking powder and salt. Create a well in the middle of the flour. Place 1 egg and the separated egg yolk in the well and beat with a fork, keeping the eggs from mixing with the flour as much as possible. With your fingers, work the butter into the eggs until well blended, then slowly mix in the sugar and lemon zest. Continue mixing without incorporating the flour until the butter and eggs are creamy.

**2** Start mixing in the flour by squeezing the ingredients together. The dough will seem dry at first, but slowly a soft ball of dough will come together. Wrap the dough in plastic wrap and chill for 30 minutes.

**3** Preheat the oven to 350°F.

**4** Lightly dust a piece of parchment paper with flour and transfer three quarters of the dough to it. Dust the top of the dough and

roll it into a 10-inch circle, dusting with more flour as needed to prevent sticking. Invert the dough into an ungreased fluted 9½-inch tart pan. Push the dough from the center toward the edges to cover the entire surface of the pan. Pass over the edges of the pan with your rolling pin to cut the fluted edges in the dough. Spread the sour cherry preserves onto the dough.

**5** Place the remaining quarter of dough on the parchment paper, dusting both heavily with flour. Roll the dough to an 8 × 10-inch rectangle ¼ inch thick. Use a pastry wheel to cut ¾-inch-wide strips of dough. Arrange the strips across the tart, leaving a ½-inch space between them, then rotate the pan slightly and place more strips on top at a 45-degree angle.

**6** Bake for 35 to 40 minutes until the filling is bubbly and the crust is deeply golden but not browned. Let cool completely before serving.

**A RUSTIC, FREE-FORM PIE** is more enjoyable to make in the summertime when fresh blueberries are as abundant as dreams of spending more time outside. I've created the dough with a mix of all-purpose and whole grain flour for a wonderful deep golden crust, and the almond cream serves as a delicious barrier between the fruit's juices and the pie dough. You can also use sliced peaches or other kinds of berries. MAKES ONE 9-INCH GALETTE

# BLUEBERRY GALETTE

### FOR THE GALETTE DOUGH

1 cup (120 g) all-purpose einkorn flour, plus more for dusting

1 cup (96 g) whole grain einkorn flour

2 tablespoons sugar, plus 1 tablespoon for sprinkling

½ teaspoon fine sea salt

7 tablespoons (97 g) cold unsalted butter, cut into ¼-inch cubes

¼ cup (59 g) ice water

### FOR THE ALMOND CREAM

¾ cup (125 g) blanched almonds (see Note)

2 tablespoons sugar

2 tablespoons unsalted butter

1 large egg, separated

### FOR THE BLUEBERRY FILLING

2 cups (260 g) fresh or frozen blueberries

¼ cup (50 g) sugar

1 tablespoon all-purpose einkorn flour

⅛ teaspoon fine sea salt

**1 MAKE THE DOUGH:** Combine the flours, the 2 tablespoons of sugar, and the salt in a medium bowl. Cut in the butter with a pastry blender until the mixture is very fine and sandy. Add the water, and mix to combine, then knead with your hands in the bowl until the dough just holds together when pressed into a ball. Form the dough into a disc, wrap in plastic wrap, and refrigerate for 30 minutes or up to 1 day. (If you chill the dough longer than 30 minutes, leave at room temperature for about 15 minutes to soften before shaping.)

**2 MAKE THE ALMOND CREAM:** Pulse the almonds and sugar in a food processor until fine. Drop in the butter and pulse for

1 minute. Add the egg yolk and pulse until the cream is as smooth as possible. Save the egg white to brush on the crust.

**3 MAKE THE FILLING:** In a medium bowl, toss together the blueberries, sugar, flour, and salt.

**4** Preheat the oven to 375°F. Dust a piece of parchment paper with flour.

**5** Remove the dough from the refrigerator and place on the parchment paper. Press on the dough with your hands to flatten, and dust the top of the dough and your rolling pin lightly with flour. Roll out the dough to a 13-inch round, lifting and turning while rolling. Transfer the dough, with the paper, to a rimmed baking sheet.

**6** Spread the almond cream on the dough, leaving a 3-inch border. Arrange the blueberry filling on top, scraping out the bowl to get all of the juices into the galette.

**7** Using the parchment paper to support it as you work, fold up and pleat the sides of the dough to form a 2½-inch border around the pie (the border should not be too tightly crimped, or the dough could tear during baking), framing the exposed blueberries in the center. Brush the crust with the reserved egg white, heavily around the pleats. Sprinkle with the 1 tablespoon sugar.

**8** Bake the galette for 52 to 54 minutes until the crust has thoroughly browned. Let cool on the pan for 30 minutes before serving. After removing the galette from the oven, spoon back any juices that may have leaked out into the center. Let cool, then use a metal spatula to slide the galette from the tray to a clean serving dish to cool completely. The galette can be stored in an airtight container at room temperature for 1 day or in the refrigerator for up to 3 days.

**NOTE:** If you can't find blanched almonds, bring a small pot of water to a boil and drop in the whole almonds for 1 minute. Drain, let cool briefly, then slip off the almond skins.

THESE DELICIOUS MINI-TARTLETS ARE gorgeous, featuring the deep orange color of ripe apricots simmered in white wine, butter, and sugar. Peaches may be substituted for the apricots; when using sweeter fruits with a tougher skin like pears or apples, be sure to reduce the sugar in the topping to 4 tablespoons, and peel the fruit first. (This recipe may also be made in a 9½-inch tart pastry pan or pie dish without any time or temperature adjustments.) I love the nontraditional technique in preparing this tart dough, which is made with melted butter, yielding a texture similar to a graham cracker crust. MAKES EIGHT 4-INCH TARTS

# APRICOT CUSTARD TARTLETS

## FOR THE DOUGH

1¾ cups (210 g) all-purpose einkorn flour

2 tablespoons sugar

¼ teaspoon fine sea salt

8 tablespoons (113 g) unsalted butter, melted

## FOR THE CUSTARD

1 large egg

¼ cup (50 g) sugar

¼ teaspoon fine sea salt

¼ cup (62 g) sour cream

¼ teaspoon pure vanilla extract

## FOR THE APRICOT TOPPING

2 tablespoons unsalted butter

1 tablespoon honey

1½ pounds (680 g) apricots (about 12), sliced in ¼-inch-thick wedges

6 tablespoons (75 g) sugar

1 tablespoon dry white wine

**1** Preheat the oven to 350°F.

**2** MAKE THE DOUGH: Mix together the flour, sugar, and salt in a medium bowl. Pour in the butter and work it into the flour mixture with your hands until the dough holds together in a firm ball. Divide the dough into 8 pieces, then press the dough evenly to fill each of the small tart pans. Prick the dough with a fork. Place the tart pans on a baking sheet and par-bake for 20 minutes, until the crust has expanded and subsided and the edges are lightly golden brown. Set aside to cool for 5 to10 minutes.

**3** MAKE THE CUSTARD: In a medium bowl, beat together the egg, sugar, and salt. Whisk in the sour cream and vanilla until well combined.

**4** MAKE THE TOPPING: In a large skillet, heat the butter and honey until the butter has melted. Arrange the apricot wedges to cover the skillet without overlapping. Sprinkle the sugar on top. Cook on high heat for 3 minutes, then add the wine and continue to cook for 3 minutes without stirring until the fruit has softened but not broken down. Add 1 tablespoon of custard to each tart. Tightly arrange the fruit on top in a circular pattern. Spoon the remaining custard and juices from the pan evenly over the tarts. Bake for 20 minutes until the custard is firm and the edges of the tarts are golden. Cool completely before serving. The tarts can be covered with plastic and stored in the refrigerator for 2 days.

**I LIVE IN A** cherry-growing region of Italy, so I created this open-faced tart to celebrate the cherries from my neighbor's farm. I prefer to use bright red cherry varieties, as opposed to the darker Bing fruit. After you invert the pan, watch your kids' faces light up at the sight of deep red cherries baked on top of the golden crust. It's best to make these in the evening, so they can cool and set overnight before removing from the pan and slicing. You may substitute frozen cherries for fresh, but the fruit will be softer. The cherry topping is slightly gooey, but you can (and should) eat these bars with your hands. MAKES 24 SQUARES

# UPSIDE-DOWN CHERRY BARS

FOR THE DOUGH

3 cups (360 g) all-purpose einkorn flour

¼ cup (50 g) sugar

½ teaspoon baking powder

½ teaspoon fine sea salt

10 tablespoons (138 g) cold unsalted butter, cut into ¼-inch cubes

2 large eggs

½ teaspoon vanilla extract

FOR THE CHERRY FILLING

2 pounds (907 g / about 6½ cups) pitted fresh cherries

⅜ cup (75 g) sugar

2 tablespoons unsalted butter

1 teaspoon dry red wine or fresh lemon juice

2 tablespoons all-purpose einkorn flour

Pinch of fine sea salt

**1** MAKE THE DOUGH: Mix together the flour, sugar, baking powder, and salt in a medium bowl. Cut the butter into the flour with a pastry blender or your hands until the mixture is coarse.

**2** In a small bowl, beat the eggs with the vanilla and 2 tablespoons cold water. Add the egg mixture to the flour mixture and squeeze the dough through your hands until it holds together in a firm ball. Wrap in plastic wrap, and refrigerate while you prepare the filling, for 30 minutes and up to 1 day. (If you chill the dough longer than 30 minutes, leave at room temperature for about 15 minutes to soften before shaping.)

**3** MAKE THE FILLING: Butter a 9 × 13-inch baking dish. Halve the pitted cherries, then place them in a large skillet with the sugar and butter and cook on medium heat for 7 minutes until softened. Add the wine or lemon juice and cook for 2 minutes. Sift the flour through a fine mesh strainer into the pan to eliminate clumps, and add the salt. Cook, stirring, for 1 to 2 minutes, until the juices thicken. Transfer the cherry mixture to the baking dish, spread out the cherries evenly with a spoon, and let cool for 15 minutes.

**4** Preheat the oven to 350°F.

**5** Remove the dough from the refrigerator and place between 2 sheets of parchment paper. Use a rolling pin to roll the dough to a 9 × 13-inch rectangle; if needed, trim the edges and reattach them to get a rectangular shape. Carefully place the dough on top of the cherries and press the edges against the dish.

**6** Bake for 40 minutes until the crust is deep golden in color. Let cool in the dish for 1 hour or overnight. Run a knife or thin spatula around the perimeter of the dish to loosen the sides, then invert over a platter. Wait a few minutes and the contents will dislodge from the dish and drop onto the platter. Cut into 2-inch squares and serve. The bars can be stored in an airtight container for up to 2 days.

**HERE IS A SIMPLE** tart made with a bit of whole grain flour for a nice golden color and slightly nutty flavor. I have filled the tart with a refreshing lemon cream, making this a nice winter or early spring treat when lemons are in season and we are all in need of some extra vitamin C.

MAKES ONE 9½-INCH TART

# LEMON CREAM TART

### FOR THE TART DOUGH

1 cup (120 g) all-purpose einkorn flour

¾ cup (72 g) whole grain einkorn flour

¼ cup (50 g) granulated sugar

¼ teaspoon fine sea salt

Zest of 1 lemon

8 tablespoons (113 g) cold unsalted butter, cut into ¼-inch cubes

2 tablespoons ice water

### FOR THE FILLING

¾ cup (150 g) granulated sugar

¼ cup (30 g) all-purpose einkorn flour

⅛ teaspoon fine sea salt

1¼ (305 g) cups whole milk

4 large egg yolks

½ cup (130 g) fresh lemon juice

Powdered sugar, for dusting

**1** MAKE THE DOUGH AND SHELL: Combine the flours, granulated sugar, and salt in a medium bowl. Stir in the lemon zest. Cut in the butter with a pastry blender until the mixture is very fine and sandy. Add the water and knead with your hands until the flour is absorbed and the dough just holds together. Form into a disc, wrap in plastic wrap, and refrigerate for 30 minutes or up to 1 day. Let the dough soften slightly before rolling.

**2** Preheat the oven to 350°F.

**3** Place the dough between 2 sheets of parchment paper. Roll out the dough to a 12-inch round that is ⅛ inch thick. Transfer the dough to a 9½-inch tart pan with a removable bottom and crimp the edges. Prick the entire shell with a fork. Bake the tart shell for 25 minutes until the shell is golden around the edges. Let cool on a wire rack for 10 minutes.

**4** MAKE THE FILLING: Combine the sugar, flour, and salt in a small bowl.

**5** In a medium saucepan over medium-low heat, bring the milk almost to a boil. Whisk the hot milk into the flour mixture until the sugar melts. Pour the wet mixture back into the pan through a fine mesh strainer and cook on medium-high heat, whisking continuously for 5 minutes until the mixture is very thick. Remove the pan from the heat and whisk in the egg yolks. Return to low heat and cook for 1 minute. Pour in the lemon juice and cook for 1 minute.

**6** Pour the lemon cream into the tart shell. Bake for 25 to 30 minutes until the lemon cream has firmed up but still jiggles a bit in the center. Cool in the pan on a rack for 30 minutes. Remove the tart from the pan, then refrigerate for at least 2 hours. Garnish with powdered sugar before serving. The tart can be stored in the refrigerator for up to 3 days.

**I LOVE SIMPLE RECIPES** that focus on einkorn and allow the whole grain's earthy flavor to shine. Here is a wholesome tart made with einkorn wheat berries that have been simmered in spiced milk for a creamy, custardy filling that is baked inside a whole grain tart shell. Soaking the wheat berries overnight beforehand creates the fluffiest texture in the custard, so I definitely recommend you do so before preparing this tart. To my delight, this is the dessert that receives raves from our guests at my cooking classes, so please give it a try. MAKES ONE 11-INCH TART

# SPICED WHEAT BERRY CUSTARD TART

### FOR THE FILLING

1¼ cups (250 g) einkorn wheat berries

2¾ cups (670 g) whole milk

¼ teaspoon fine sea salt

2 whole cardamom pods

1 bay leaf

2 whole cloves

4 tablespoons (60 g) unsalted butter

3 large eggs

½ cup (110 g) (packed) dark brown sugar

### FOR THE TART DOUGH

2 cups (192 g) whole grain einkorn flour, plus more for dusting

2 tablespoons granulated sugar

¼ teaspoon fine sea salt

6 tablespoons (90 g) cold unsalted butter, cut into ¼-inch cubes, plus more for greasing the pan

1 large egg yolk

2 tablespoons cold whole milk

**1** MAKE THE FILLING: Place the wheat berries in a medium bowl, cover with 3 cups of water, and soak for 8 hours. Drain and rinse.

**2** In a medium saucepan, bring the milk to a boil over medium heat. Add the wheat berries and salt. Place the cardamom, bay leaf, and cloves in a sachet or tea strainer and add to the pot. Simmer gently for 30 minutes over low heat, stirring frequently. Stir in the butter and let cool for 15 minutes. Remove the spice sachet, then beat in the eggs and brown sugar. (It is not

recommended to make the filling in advance or the wheat berries will continue to absorb the liquid, making the tart dry after baking.)

**3** MAKE THE DOUGH AND SHELL: Mix together the flour, granulated sugar, and salt in a large bowl. Cut in the butter with a pastry blender until the mixture is very fine and sandy, with chunks of butter broken up into the flour.

**4** In a small bowl, mix together the egg yolk and milk. Add to the flour mixture and squeeze the mixture through your hands until it holds together. Form into a disc, wrap in plastic, and

refrigerate for 30 minutes or up to 1 day. (If you chill the dough longer than 30 minutes, leave at room temperature for about 15 minutes to soften before rolling out.)

5  Preheat the oven to 350°F. Butter an 11-inch tart pan.

6  Place the dough between 2 sheets of parchment paper. Use your rolling pin to roll out the dough to a ⅛-thick round that is 12 inches in diameter. Press the dough into

the tart pan and crimp the sides, trimming the excess.

7  Pour the spiced filling into the shell and place the tart pan on top of a baking sheet to catch any drips. Bake for 45 minutes until the edges are golden brown. Place the pan on a rack to cool completely before serving at room temperature. The tart can be stored in an airtight container in the refrigerator for up to 5 days. Serve at room temperature or chilled.

**WHILE ITALIANS LIKE THEIR** cookies and cakes on the dry and crunchy side, Americans tend to prefer soft and chewy. By adding sour cream, I have softened up a very crunchy traditional Italian tart—really a cross between a cookie and a simple cake—that is referred to as "the crumbly one," or *sbrisolona,* in the city of Mantova. I love this type of ancient rustic baking because the ingredients are simple and they all come together quickly with no need to worry about technique. To serve, invert the tart onto a platter and let everyone break off pieces with their hands, accompanied by a glass of wine or a cup of tea. MAKES ONE 11-INCH TART

# ALMOND CRUNCH TART

1 cup (120 g) all-purpose einkorn flour

1 cup (96 g) whole grain einkorn flour

1 cup (112 g) almond flour

1 cup (115 g) fine grind cornmeal

1 cup (95 g) coarsely ground almonds

1 cup (200 g) sugar

¼ teaspoon fine sea salt

10 tablespoons (138 g) cold unsalted butter, cut into ¼-inch cubes

2 large egg yolks

⅓ cup (76 g) sour cream

**1** Preheat the oven to 350°F. Lightly grease an 11-inch tart pan.

**2** In a large bowl, mix together the three flours, cornmeal, almonds, sugar, and salt. Cut in the butter with a pastry blender until the mixture is very fine and sandy, with the chunks of butter broken up into the flour.

**3** In a small bowl, beat together the yolks and sour cream. Stir the egg mixture into the flour mixture. Using your hands, squeeze the dough together until no dry flour is visible and the dough clumps together.

**4** Drop handfuls of dough into the tart pan. Press the mixture with your fingers to cover the pan completely, leaving the indentations of your fingers.

**5** Bake the tart for 45 to 50 minutes until the edges are browned and the top is deeply golden. Let cool to room temperature, then invert onto a platter to serve. The cake can be stored in an airtight container at room temperature for up to 5 days.

**IF YOU HAVE EVER** visited a pastry shop in Italy, you surely know that these cream puffs, or *bigne,* are presented in many ways—filled with pastry cream, whipped cream, chocolate cream, and *gianduja* (hazelnut) cream. This recipe is fun and fairly easy with guaranteed good results for profiteroles filled with either cream or gelato, or chocolate éclairs. The filling can also be savory.

MAKES 12 CREAM PUFFS

# ITALIAN CREAM PUFFS

FOR THE DOUGH

¼ cup (60 g) whole milk

4 tablespoons (56 g) unsalted butter

1 teaspoon granulated sugar

¼ teaspoon fine sea salt

¼ cup (60 g) water

1 cup (120 g) all-purpose einkorn flour

3 large eggs

FOR THE PASTRY CREAM FILLING

½ cup (100 g) granulated sugar

¼ cup (30 g) all-purpose einkorn flour

Pinch of salt

1½ cups (366 g) whole milk

3 large egg yolks

Powdered sugar, for dusting

**1** Preheat the oven to 375°F. Line a baking sheet with parchment paper. Fit a pastry bag with a 1-inch round tip.

**2** MAKE THE DOUGH: In a medium saucepan, combine the milk, butter, granulated sugar, salt, and water and bring almost to a boil over medium heat. Stir until the butter and sugar have melted. Sift in the flour all at once. Continue to cook over medium heat, maintaining the mixture at a temperature just below boiling, stirring vigorously with a wooden spoon, until the mixture will leave the sides of the pan and form a stiff ball fairly quickly. Continue to cook and stir for 2 minutes. If the dough is too hard to stir, press on it with the spoon. Be careful not to let the mixture get hot enough to bubble or brown.

**3** Transfer the dough to the bowl of a standing mixer, and let cool for 5 minutes. Add 1 of the eggs and mix on medium speed until the dough goes from clumpy to smooth, about 30 seconds. Continue with the remaining 2 eggs in the same manner.

**4** Fill the pastry bag with the dough and pipe out rounds that are about 2 inches in diameter and about ¾ inch tall on the baking sheet. Space the pastries 2 inches apart on the tray. Bake for 35 minutes until golden brown. Cool the cream puffs on a wire rack for 15 minutes.

**5** MAKE THE CREAM FILLING: Mix together the granulated sugar, flour, and salt in a medium heatproof bowl. Heat the milk in a medium saucepan until almost boiling. Whisk ¼ cup of milk into the flour mixture and beat until the mixture is smooth. Slowly whisk in the remaining 1¼ cups of milk. Pour the wet

mixture back into the pan, and cook over medium-low heat for 5 minutes, stirring vigorously, until thick and smooth. It will start out very thin but will firm up. Whisk in the egg yolks and continue to cook for 5 minutes, stirring frequently. Pour into a bowl and allow to cool completely, stirring occasionally, until the pastry cream is firm.

**6** You may either slice the pastries in half and fill with 2 tablespoons of cream or puncture a hole in the side with a skewer and pipe in the cream using a pastry bag fitted with a ¼-inch plain tip. Dust with powdered sugar. Serve within 2 to 3 hours at room temperature, or store in an airtight container in the refrigerator for up to 1 day and serve chilled.

**WHILE THE RICE PUDDING** of my youth was pale white and soft, this lightly sweetened version made with einkorn berries has an earthy color from the whole grain and a characteristically chewy consistency. Have patience when cooking the custard—if you raise the heat too high while the custard thickens, you will have scrambled eggs. The pudding may not seem thick enough at first, but after chilling it will set into a wholesome yet pleasing dessert. SERVES 6

# EINKORN "RICE" PUDDING

3 cups (735 g) whole milk

½ cup (100 g) einkorn wheat berries

⅛ teaspoon fine sea salt

3 large eggs

2 bay leaves

1 whole clove

½ vanilla bean

¼ cup (50 g) sugar

**1** In a small saucepan, bring 1 cup of the milk almost to a boil slowly over medium-low heat, about 8 minutes. Add the wheat berries and salt and simmer on very low heat, covered, for 35 minutes until the wheat berries are tender, stirring occasionally. Remove from the heat and let stand, covered, for 5 minutes.

**2** Beat the eggs together in a medium bowl.

**3** Add the remaining 2 cups of milk to a medium saucepan. Place the bay leaves and clove in a sachet or tea strainer and add to the pot. Slice open the vanilla bean and scrape out the seeds into the milk. Then drop in the pod. Warm over low heat until just about boiling, about 8 minutes. Slowly whisk ¼ cup of the warm milk into the beaten eggs, a spoonful at a time, until tempered, then pour the warmed eggs into the saucepan with the milk mixture.

**4** Add the wheat berry mixture to the medium saucepan, then whisk in the sugar and continue stirring. Cook on low heat until the mixture begins to thicken and coats the back of a spoon like yogurt, stirring constantly, 15 to 20 minutes. The mixture should not bubble, but steam should just barely rise off the surface. Remove the spice sachet and vanilla pod.

**5** Fill small serving bowls or glasses with the pudding, about ½ cup per serving. Let cool, then cover with plastic wrap and refrigerate overnight before serving. The pudding may be stored in an airtight container in the refrigerator for 3 days.

# PIZZA, PASTA
## & SAVORY MAIN DISHES

NEAPOLITAN PIZZA
MARGHERITA

WHOLE GRAIN KALE
PESTO PIZZA

NEW YORK–STYLE PIZZA

WHOLE GRAIN TAGLIATELLE
WITH PAN-FRIED CHERRY
TOMATOES

SPINACH LASAGNA
BOLOGNESE

BUTTERNUT SQUASH GNOCCHI
& TOMATO SAUCE

FRESH RICOTTA TORTELLONI

BRAISING GREENS PIE

ROASTED ROOT VEGETABLE &
CHICKEN COUNTRY-STYLE PIE

TUSCAN FARRO SOUP

BEEF SPEZZATINO WITH
EINKORN POLENTA

COD & SALMON BURGERS

Neapolitan Pizza Margherita, page 169

**THE BEST PIZZA I EVER TASTED WAS IN NAPLES,** and for good reason. True Neapolitan pizza dough is fermented slowly for many hours for the best flavor. The climate in southern Italy is probably the best in the world for growing naturally sweet tomatoes that contain lots of pulp under the skin. Local cheese makers are renowned for their fresh mozzarella, especially when made with buffalo milk. Whether you prefer a classic margherita, sourdough whole grain, or New York–style pizza, all of these are covered in this chapter's collection of my favorite savory dishes.

I learned how to make fresh pasta from the older generation, and I can attest to the authenticity of my favorite pasta, Fresh Ricotta Tortelloni (page 183). Making fresh einkorn pasta is not difficult—it just takes some adjustments in the amount of flour used. I recommend using a hand-cranked pasta machine, as my attempts with ravioli attachments or pasta extruders on the standing mixer were very frustrating.

Braising Greens Pie (page 185) is how I got my children to love greens, and that pie is served for dinner in our home quite frequently during the colder months, normally accompanied by a bowl of vegetable soup. It is made with a lighter olive oil crust, so it is a nice alternative to buttery crusts. The crust I use for Roasted Root Vegetable & Chicken Country-Style Pie

(page 186) can also be used for quiche. You might not have a lot of einkorn bread leftover for bread crumbs, but when I do I love to make Cod & Salmon Burgers (page 193), especially in the summer when I have fresh dill in the garden.

I hope your pantry remains stocked with whole einkorn wheat berries. They are an essential ingredient for many dishes, like Tuscan Farro Soup (page 189) and Beef Spezzatino with Einkorn Polenta (page 190) in this chapter. They also make a great side dish topped with melted butter or tomato sauce. I also like to add wheat berries to my Caesar salad instead of croutons. What a delicious way to cut back on saturated fat while enjoying a plentiful helping of protein and fiber.

WHILE THE ORIGINS OF pizza itself may be uncertain, the margherita pizza was created in 1889 especially for Queen Margherita's visit to the city of Naples. The pizza was made in the colors of the Italian flag, represented by tomato, mozzarella, and basil. Real margherita pizza is made with a very slow fermentation and no oil in the dough. The pizza should be spread out thin and then slid onto a hot surface to bake at the oven's maximum temperature for just a few minutes. To get an authentically thin crust using einkorn flour in the dough, you may need to use a rolling pin, in addition to your hands. Plan to mix the dough and let it rest at least 8 hours at room temperature or for up to 24 hours in the refrigerator. Since the tomatoes are not cooked into a sauce before topping the pizza, you will need a high-quality product for this pizza, preferably tomatoes packed in glass like jovial organic crushed tomatoes (photograph on page 166). MAKES SIX 9-INCH PIZZAS

# NEAPOLITAN PIZZA MARGHERITA

FOR THE DOUGH

¼ cup (60 g) refreshed Einkorn Sourdough Starter (page 13), or ¼ teaspoon active dry yeast

1¼ cups (295 g) warm water, at 100°F

4¾ cups (570 g) all-purpose einkorn flour, plus more for dusting

2½ teaspoons fine sea salt

FOR THE TOPPING

1½ cups jarred crushed tomatoes

2 tablespoons extra-virgin olive oil

½ teaspoon fine sea salt

12 ounces fresh mozzarella, thinly sliced

1 cup fresh basil leaves

1 MAKE THE DOUGH: In a large bowl, combine the starter or yeast with the water. Mix gently with a fork until the mixture becomes creamy. Add the flour, sprinkle the salt on top, and begin to mix the dough with a spatula as much as you can, then squeeze the dough through your hands until it holds together.

2 Generously flour a work surface and transfer the dough to it. Knead for 2 minutes until the dough is very smooth and a bit sticky. Place back in the bowl, cover tightly with plastic wrap, and place a kitchen towel over the bowl. Let proof at room temperature for 8 to 12 hours or in the refrigerator for up to 24 hours.

(continues)

**3** Dust a baking sheet lightly with flour. Divide the dough into 6 pieces. Lightly flour a work surface and roll each piece of dough into a tight ball on the work area. Place the dough balls on the prepared baking sheet and cover tightly with oiled plastic wrap. Let proof at room temperature for 1 hour.

**4** Place 2 baking sheets in the oven. Preheat the oven to 500°F for 30 minutes.

**5** MAKE THE TOPPING: In a medium bowl, combine the tomatoes, oil, and salt. Set aside.

**6** To form small round pizzas: Stretch one ball of dough out to a 6-inch round by hand. Heavily dust a piece of parchment paper with flour and place the dough round on it. Flour the top and cover with another piece of parchment. With a rolling pin, roll the round to a disc 9 inches in diameter. Lift up the paper and use your hands to gently form a raised edge around the outside of the round. Slide the dough onto one of the preheated baking sheets. Add $\frac{1}{4}$ cup of the tomato sauce to the center of the pizza. Use the back of a spoon to spread it out evenly in a circular motion. Top with mozzarella and basil leaves.

**7** Bake the pizzas two sheets at a time for 6 to 8 minutes until the edges are dark golden brown and crispy. Serve the pizzas hot out of the oven and proceed with making the remaining pizzas in the same manner.

NOTE: If you are using a pizza stone, preheat it at 500°F for 60 minutes while the dough proofs and use a floured pizza peel to transfer the pizza to the stone.

IF YOU HAVE MADE pizza with modern wheat flour or watched a professional pizzaiolo toss and spin the dough in the air, then you know how strong gluten can be. The gluten in today's soft wheat lends incredible elasticity to pizza dough, but that strong network of gluten proteins can also weigh on your digestion. With einkorn pizza dough, especially whole grain, you will need to have patience when stretching out the dough because with its weaker gluten the dough will tear easily. Whole grain einkorn pizza is softer because it contains more fiber and it has a pleasingly nutty flavor that pairs well with kale pesto. My daughter loves to add a slice of smoked salmon right at the table. MAKES SIX 9-INCH INDIVIDUAL PIZZAS OR 2 THICK-CRUST PIZZAS

# WHOLE GRAIN KALE PESTO PIZZA

## FOR THE PIZZA

¼ cup (60 g) refreshed Einkorn Sourdough Starter (page 13), or ¼ teaspoon active dry yeast

1½ cups (354 g) warm water, at 100°F

6 cups (576 g) whole grain einkorn flour, plus more for dusting

2½ teaspoons fine sea salt

## FOR THE TOPPING

1 pound (454 g) dinosaur kale, stems removed

2 teaspoons fine sea salt

2 garlic cloves

¼ cup (50 g) extra-virgin olive oil

½ cup (50 g) grated pecorino Romano cheese

1 cup cooked cannellini beans (optional)

12 ounces (340 g) fresh burrata mozzarella, thinly sliced

1 MAKE THE PIZZA: In a large bowl, gently mix the starter or yeast and water with a fork until the mixture becomes creamy. Add the flour, sprinkle the salt on top, and begin to mix the dough together in the bowl by squeezing the mixture through your hands until the dough holds together. Cover the bowl with a plate and let rest for 15 minutes. Lightly flour a work surface and transfer the dough onto it. Knead for 2 minutes until very smooth and a bit sticky. Return the dough to the bowl, cover with plastic wrap, and place a kitchen towel over the bowl. Let proof at room temperature for 8 to 12 hours or in the refrigerator for up to 24 hours.

2 Dust a baking sheet lightly with flour. For individual round pizzas, divide the dough into 6 pieces. For sheet pizzas, divide the dough into 2 pieces. Lightly flour a work surface and

(continues)

roll each piece into a tight ball on the work area. Place the dough balls on the prepared baking sheet and cover tightly with oiled plastic wrap. Let proof at room temperature for 30 minutes.

**3** **MAKE THE TOPPING:** Cook the kale in a pot of boiling water with 1 teaspoon of the salt for 7 minutes. Lift out the greens into a colander, without squeezing out the water. Add to a food processor with the garlic, oil, the remaining teaspoon of salt, and the grated cheese. Process until the pesto is smooth. The pesto can be stored in the refrigerator for up to 2 days.

**4** Place 2 baking sheets in the oven. Preheat the oven to 500°F for 30 minutes.

**5** To form round pizzas, stretch the first piece of dough out to a 6-inch round by hand. Heavily dust a piece of parchment paper with flour. Place the dough on the floured parchment paper, flour the top, and cover with another piece of parchment. With a rolling pin, roll the dough into a round 9 inches in diameter. Lift up the paper and use your hands to gently form a raised edge around the outside of the round. Slide the dough onto one of the preheated baking sheets. Add 3 to 4 tablespoons of the pesto to the center of the pizza. Use the back of a spoon to spread it out evenly in a circular motion. Top with 2 tablespoons of beans, if using, and mozzarella. Roll out the remaining pizzas in the same manner. Bake the pizzas for 9 to 10 minutes until the edges are darkened and crisp.

**6** If you are making thick-crust pizza, spread out one of the larger balls of dough to fit a half sheet pan. Bake the pizza shell for 7 minutes, and then spread half of the pesto, beans, and cheese on the pizza. Bake for 8 to 10 minutes more until the edges darken.

**7** Serve the pizzas hot out of the oven.

**NOTE:** If you are using a pizza stone, preheat it at 500°F for 60 minutes while the dough proofs and use a floured pizza peel to transfer the pizza to the stone.

I CALL THIS NEW York–Style Pizza to distinguish it from Italy's Neapolitan pizza. It has a thicker crust, which can support more sauce, cheese, and toppings. It is quite easy to spread this dough out to an 8-inch round using your hands, but remember that you should push out from the center of the round to transfer the air pockets to the edges so you will get that characteristically bubbly crust. This recipe is made with more yeast and only needs to proof for a little more than 2 hours before baking, but you may extend that by refrigerating the dough. MAKES FOUR 8-INCH PIZZAS

# NEW YORK–STYLE PIZZA

FOR THE DOUGH

1¼ cups (295 g) warm water, at 100°F

1 teaspoon active dry yeast

1 teaspoon sugar

5 cups (600 g) all-purpose einkorn flour, plus more for dusting

2 teaspoons fine sea salt

3 tablespoons extra-virgin olive oil, plus more for greasing the pan

FOR THE TOPPING

2 tablespoons unsalted butter

2 tablespoons extra-virgin olive oil

1 small onion, minced

2 garlic cloves, minced

4 cups (36 ounces) jarred whole peeled tomatoes

2 tablespoons tomato paste

½ teaspoon dried oregano

½ teaspoon dried basil

12 ounces (340 g) mozzarella cheese, shredded

1 MAKE THE DOUGH: In a large bowl, mix together the water, yeast, sugar, and 1 cup (120 g) of the flour. Let stand for 15 minutes until the mixture begins to bubble. Add the remaining 4 cups (480 g) flour and the salt and mix together as much as you can with a stiff spatula. Add the oil and begin kneading the dough in the bowl until it holds together. Lightly flour a work surface. Turn out the dough onto the work area and knead for 2 to 3 minutes until smooth. Place the dough back in the bowl and cover tightly with plastic wrap. Let rest for 2 hours at room temperature until the dough rises by 30 percent. (You may also let the dough proof in the refrigerator for up to 8 hours.)

2 MAKE THE TOPPING: Heat the butter and oil on medium heat in a large saucepan. Add the onion and garlic and cook for 1 minute, being careful not to let it brown. Add the tomatoes, tomato paste, oregano, and basil and cook uncovered for 1 hour, breaking down the tomatoes with a wooden spoon as they cook.

3 Lightly grease a baking sheet with oil. Divide the dough into 4 pieces. Roll each piece into a tight ball and place on the prepared baking sheet. Cover the dough with lightly oiled plastic wrap. Let rest for 15 minutes. (At this point, you may freeze the balls of dough for up to 1 month in sealed plastic bags, then thaw and bake at a later date.)

**4** Place 2 baking sheets in the oven. Preheat the oven to 500°F for 30 minutes.

**5** Heavily dust a piece of parchment paper with flour and place a ball of dough on it. Use your hands to gently stretch the dough into an 8-inch round. Gently form a ¾-inch raised edge around the outside of the round. Slide the dough onto one of the preheated baking sheets. Repeat with the remaining pieces of dough.

**6** Add 1 cup of sauce to each crust, spreading evenly to the raised edge with the back of a spoon. Sprinkle a quarter of the cheese over the sauce.

**7** Bake the pizzas for 10 to 12 minutes until the edges are dark brown and the cheese just begins to brown. Serve the pizzas immediately, hot out of the oven.

**NOTE:** If you are using a pizza stone, preheat it at 500°F for 60 minutes while the dough proofs and use a floured pizza peel to transfer the pizza to the stone.

AFTER ALL OF THESE years of cooking with einkorn, I am still amazed at how delicious the whole grain tastes in all types of recipes. Fresh pasta made with regular whole wheat flour has a gritty texture, but whole grain einkorn is sweet, nutty, and delicate in both flavor and texture. Letting the dough rest will allow the flour to absorb some moisture so it will roll out nicely in your pasta machine. The drying time can vary depending on the size of your eggs and the temperature in your kitchen, but the finished pasta can be kept frozen for up to a month, or dried and stored for up to a week, wrapped in parchment paper. SERVES 6

# WHOLE GRAIN TAGLIATELLE WITH PAN-FRIED CHERRY TOMATOES

### FOR THE PASTA

4 cups (384 g) whole grain einkorn flour, plus more for dusting

4 large eggs

1 tablespoon fine sea salt, for cooking the pasta

### FOR THE SAUCE

2 pounds (900 g) cherry tomatoes, halved (about 6 cups)

3 tablespoons extra-virgin olive oil

2 garlic cloves, minced

1 teaspoon fine sea salt

¼ teaspoon crushed red pepper flakes

1 cup fresh basil leaves

¾ cup (3 ounces/85 g) ricotta salata or pecorino Romano cheese, shaved

1 MAKE THE PASTA: Add the flour to a large bowl and create a well in the center. Add the eggs to the well and beat with a fork until the yolks and whites are combined. Slowly mix in the flour from the sides of the bowl until the mixture becomes stiff. Knead in the bowl by squeezing the dough through your hands. When the dough begins to come together, lightly dust your work surface with flour and transfer the dough to it.

2 Knead the dough for 1 to 2 minutes by pressing down with both hands while rolling the dough away from you until it is smooth. Place in the bowl and cover with a plate and let rest for 15 minutes.

3 Divide the dough into 4 pieces and press the first piece into a 4 × 1½-inch rectangle that is about ¾ inch thick. Dust the first piece with flour on both sides. Start with the thickest setting on your pasta machine and roll it through the machine. The piece will break up, but fold the piece in thirds lengthwise and pass it through the machine, repeating it until you have a uniform strip. With a knife, trim the edges to be straight, then cut the strip in three equal pieces lengthwise. Pass the dough through the machine, working down to the second-to-last thickness. Pass the strips through this setting twice, then place the strips of dough on clean kitchen towels to dry for 30 minutes, until the pasta has lost its stickiness but is still flexible and not stiff. If the

strips become too dry, they will be difficult to cut.

4 Pass each strip of dough through the tagliatelle die of your pasta machine. Spread the pasta out on the kitchen towels and let it dry until you are ready to cook it or dry it completely before storing.

5 **MAKE THE SAUCE:** Add the tomatoes, olive oil, garlic, salt, and red pepper flakes to a large skillet. Turn the heat to high and cook for 10 minutes until the tomatoes have wilted but still hold their shape. Add the basil and cook for 30 seconds until the basil has just wilted. Remove the skillet from the heat and add the cheese.

6 To cook the pasta, bring 3 quarts of water to a rolling boil in a large pot. Add the salt. Drop in the tagliatelle and cover the pot to bring the water up to a rolling boil. Once boiling, cook uncovered for 1 to 2 minutes until the noodles are al dente. Drain the noodles in a colander, but do not rinse.

7 Heat the sauce to high, and add the noodles directly to the skillet, stirring with kitchen tongs until the noodles have absorbed the tomato sauce, about 2 minutes. Serve right away.

BOLOGNA WAS THE FIRST Italian city that I fell in love with, and I lived there for two years. I loved to walk through the streets and visit the endless number of small family-owned food shops. The owners of each little neighborhood vegetable, cheese, meat, and fish shop were all expert advisers and recipe providers to their faithful clientele. One of the best-known dishes of Bologna is lasagna, which is made with meat and béchamel sauce and fresh spinach pasta. The layers are sprinkled with freshly grated Parmigiano cheese, never mozzarella. The lasagna bakes up in thinner layers than the ricotta-filled lasagna of southern Italy, and the flavor is amazing. Once you assemble the lasagna, you may refrigerate the dish and bake it the following day. MAKES ONE 9 × 13-INCH LASAGNA

# SPINACH LASAGNA BOLOGNESE

### FOR THE MEAT SAUCE

½ medium onion, minced

3 tablespoons extra-virgin olive oil

½ pound (227 g) ground beef

½ pound (227 g) ground pork

¼ pound (114 g) ground veal

1 sprig of fresh rosemary

3 tablespoons red or white wine

1 teaspoon fine sea salt

4 cups jarred crushed or diced tomatoes

### FOR THE LASAGNA NOODLES

½ pound (227 g) fresh spinach, trimmed

3½ cups (420 g) all-purpose einkorn flour, plus more for dusting

3 large eggs

1 tablespoon fine sea salt, for cooking the noodles

### FOR THE BÉCHAMEL SAUCE

5 tablespoons (62 g) unsalted butter

½ cup (60 g) all-purpose einkorn flour

¼ teaspoon fine sea salt

3 cups (732 g) hot whole milk

1½ cups (3.5 ounces/100 g) finely grated Parmigiano-Reggiano

**1** MAKE THE MEAT SAUCE: Sauté the onion in the oil on low heat in a large saucepan for 2 to 3 minutes. Add the beef, pork, veal, and rosemary and cook on medium heat until the meat is browned throughout, about 10 minutes, stirring frequently. Remove the sprig of rosemary. Pour in the wine and salt and let cook for 2 minutes. Add the tomatoes and simmer uncovered on medium-low heat for 1 hour, stirring occasionally. Be careful to maintain the sauce at bubbling but not boiling.

**2** **MAKE THE PASTA:** Steam the spinach in a basket steamer until tender, about 3 minutes. Drain and let cool completely. Squeeze the spinach to remove all of the excess water and chop as finely as possible.

**3** In a large bowl, add the flour and create a well in the middle. Add the eggs and spinach into the well and beat them together with a fork until combined. Slowly incorporate the flour into the egg mixture using the fork. Knead with your hands until you have a shaggy dough that starts to hold together. Lightly flour a work surface and transfer the dough to it. Knead the dough by hand for 2 minutes until it is completely smooth and slightly sticky. Form a tight ball and transfer to the bowl and keep covered with plastic wrap.

**4** Separate the dough into 6 equal pieces and remove 1 piece, leaving the rest of the dough covered in the bowl so it does not dry out. Use your hands to press the dough into a 4 × 2½-inch rectangle. Dust both sides of the pasta with flour. Starting with the thickest setting, pass the dough, short side first, through the pasta machine once. Cut the strip of pasta into three equal pieces lengthwise. Continue to pass the dough through the pasta machine, dropping down a setting until you arrive at the second-from-last setting, dusting the pasta with flour between rolling if necessary. Place the strip of dough on a clean kitchen towel to dry. Continue in the same manner with the remaining dough, and let the pasta dry for 1 hour.

**5** **MAKE THE BÉCHAMEL:** Melt the butter in a medium saucepan. Stir in the flour and salt and cook for 30 seconds, whisking constantly. Slowly add the hot milk, ½ cup at a time, whisking after each addition until the mixture is smooth and thickens. Cook on medium heat, whisking constantly, for about 4 minutes until the mixture has thickened to a gravy consistency. Remove from the heat.

**6** To assemble the lasagna, bring 3 quarts of water to a boil in a large pot with the salt. Drop 3 noodles into the boiling water and cook for 1 minute. The noodles will not cook completely but will become flexible. Lift out the noodles with a skimmer and place them on a clean kitchen towel. Cover the bottom of the pan with a thin layer of meat sauce. Arrange three noodles into a single layer without being concerned about overlapping. Add ¾ cup of the meat sauce and spread evenly over the noodles. Add ½ cup of the béchamel and spread over the meat sauce, then top with ¼ cup of the cheese. Continue in this manner for 6 layers, finishing with the cheese. To store the lasagna for up to one day before baking, cover tightly with plastic wrap and refrigerate.

**7** Cover the pan with aluminum foil. Preheat the oven to 375°F. Bake for 40 minutes, then remove the foil and bake for 10 to 15 additional minutes until the noodles begin to brown on top. Remove from the oven and let rest for 10 to 15 minutes, then slice and serve right away. Leftovers may be refrigerated for up to 3 days and reheated at 375°F for 10 minutes before serving.

ADDING A BIT OF butternut squash to classic potato gnocchi really lightens them up, and lends a warming color and flavor. My Italian mother-in-law insists on including a bit of grappa in the dough, so the alcohol can act as a leavener, which makes the gnocchi even lighter. I agree, but there is no need to run out and buy grappa—you can use vodka instead, or just omit it from the recipe. The gnocchi will be light and tender without it, as long as you refrain from adding too much extra flour. The dough is a bit tricky to work with, so save the flour for when you really need it during shaping. As the flour slowly absorbs the liquids from the potato and squash, the gnocchi can become wet and stick together. Therefore, if you are not going to cook the gnocchi right after you finish rolling them, I recommend freezing them after shaping. SERVES 4

# BUTTERNUT SQUASH GNOCCHI & TOMATO SAUCE

FOR THE GNOCCHI

2 cups (260 g) peeled and ½-inch diced butternut squash

2 cups (260 g) peeled and ¼-inch diced yellow potatoes

½ teaspoon grappa (optional)

2¾ cups (330 g) all-purpose einkorn flour, plus more for dusting

1 tablespoon fine sea salt, for cooking the gnocchi

FOR THE TOMATO SAUCE

18 ounces (520 g) jarred crushed or diced tomatoes

1 small onion, quartered

2 tablespoons extra-virgin olive oil

1 teaspoon fine sea salt

6 fresh basil leaves

Grated Parmigiano-Reggiano, for serving

1 MAKE THE GNOCCHI: Steam the squash and potatoes in a large pot fitted with a basket steamer, cooking for 12 minutes until the pieces can be pierced easily with a knife. Remove the steaming tray from the pan, and let drain and cool for 10 minutes. Pass the potatoes and squash through a potato ricer or food mill fitted with a middle-holed disc into a large bowl. Drizzle with grappa, if using. Add the flour and squeeze the dough in your hands until the flour is absorbed. Lightly dust your work surface with flour

and transfer the dough to it. Knead the dough until it begins to stick. Transfer to the bowl and cover with plastic wrap. Let stand for 15 minutes.

2 Dust 2 trays that will fit in your freezer with flour.

3 Divide the dough into 8 pieces. Dust your work surface with 1 tablespoon of flour. Working with 1 piece of dough at a time, gently press and roll out the dough with your hands to form a

long rope that is 18 inches long and ½ inch in diameter. The strip of dough should be covered with flour. Cut into 1-inch-long pieces. Turn a fork over, and roll each piece from the top of the arch to the tip of the fork, pressing with your index finger to make an indentation on the underside of the gnocchi. Place the gnocchi in the freezer, making sure to keep them apart so they do not stick. Freeze them uncovered on the tray until cooking, or transfer them to a sealed plastic bag once they have hardened and freeze for up to 1 month.

4 **MAKE THE SAUCE:** Combine the tomatoes, onion, oil, and salt in a medium skillet. Simmer on medium-low heat for 20 minutes uncovered. Turn off the heat; remove the pieces of onion and stir in the basil leaves.

5 In a large pot, bring 3 quarts of water to a rolling boil and add the salt. Lift up the gnocchi from the tray with a spatula and drop into the pot. Bring back to a full boil. Cook for 3 to 4 minutes until the gnocchi are soft but still have some bite in the center. Drain and serve right away, topped with the tomato sauce and grated cheese.

**THIS RECIPE PAYS HOMAGE** to Emilia-Romagna, a region of Italy where I have spent many years with my husband and children. I originally met my husband during my junior year abroad in Bologna, an amazing city to land in if you love food. Whenever I had the opportunity while there, I spent time in the kitchen talking and learning from the older women I met, which is how I learned to make tortelloni. I will be honest in saying this dish will take some time to prepare, but authentic tortelloni taste so good with melted butter and sage, it will be worth the effort. We like to set up a little assembly line with our children, with one adult rolling out the pasta while the others shape the tortelloni. SERVES 6; MAKES ABOUT 100 TORTELLONI

# FRESH RICOTTA TORTELLONI

### FOR THE FILLING

½ pound (225 g) Swiss chard, leaves stripped from the stems, or baby spinach (see Note)

1 large egg

15 ounces (425 g) whole milk ricotta cheese

1¼ cups (4.5 ounces/125 g) finely grated Parmigiano-Reggiano cheese

1 teaspoon fine sea salt

### FOR THE PASTA

3 cups (360 g) all-purpose einkorn flour, plus more for dusting

4 large eggs

1 tablespoon fine sea salt, for cooking the tortelloni

### FOR THE SAUCE

8 tablespoons (113 g) unsalted butter

15 fresh sage leaves

Parmigiano-Reggiano cheese, for serving

**1** MAKE THE FILLING: Bring a large stockpot of water to a rolling boil and cook the Swiss chard or spinach for 5 minutes until very tender, then drain and let cool. Squeeze all of the water out of the greens with your hands and then mince as finely as possible with a sharp knife.

**2** In a medium bowl, beat the egg. Add the ricotta, Parmigiano-Reggiano, and salt, and mix until the ingredients are incorporated. Add the chard and continue to mix with a fork until the greens are evenly distributed throughout the filling—the filling should

taste very sharp and salty. You can hold the filling in the refrigerator, tightly wrapped, for up to 1 day.

**3** MAKE THE PASTA: Add the flour to a large bowl and form a well in the center. Beat the eggs in the well. Mix in the flour gradually with a fork, then knead in the bowl until the dough starts to hold together. Lightly dust a work surface with flour and transfer the dough to it. Knead the dough until smooth, then place it in a bowl and cover the bowl with plastic wrap so the dough does not dry out.

(continues)

**4** Cut the dough into 12 equal pieces. Working 1 piece of dough at a time, leaving the rest covered in the bowl tightly with plastic wrap, form the dough into a 4 × 2-inch rectangle. Dust the pasta on both sides with flour. Starting with the thickest setting, pass the dough, wide side first, through your pasta machine once at each setting until you arrive at the second-from-last setting, dusting with flour as necessary. Pass the strip of pasta through this setting twice.

**5** Flour your work surface and lay down the long strip of dough. Cut it into 2½-inch squares. Place 1 teaspoon of filling in the center; fold over one side to form a triangle, making sure to seal the edges by pressing hard on the dough. Bring the opposite points of the triangle together to form a circle at the bottom of the triangle, twisting the loop of the circle you have formed before pinching the ends together to seal. Set on a floured surface and proceed with the other strips of dough.

**6** Line a tray or platter that will fit in your freezer with parchment paper, and lightly dust with flour. Place the tortelloni on the tray or platter so they are not touching and place in the freezer when full. As soon as the tortelloni harden, transfer them to a freezer bag and keep working.

**7** **MAKE THE SAUCE:** Melt the butter in a large skillet with the sage leaves, then turn up the heat until the butter begins to sizzle but not brown, about 2 minutes. Add to a large serving platter.

**8** To cook the tortelloni, bring 3 quarts of water to a rolling boil in a medium stockpot, and season with the salt. Drop in the tortelloni and gently stir with a slotted spoon. Cover and let come to a boil, then remove the lid and cook for 4 to 5 minutes until the pasta is tender.

**9** Remove the tortelloni with a slotted spoon from the water, taking care to drain well, then transfer them to a serving bowl and cover with the butter and sage dressing, gently mixing until well seasoned. Top with grated Parmigiano-Reggiano and serve.

**NOTE:** Using young chard is preferred, but baby spinach can also be substituted. Rainbow chard is not suited to this recipe.

IN ITALY, THIS TYPE of savory pie is normally made with lard, but I like to use olive oil instead. The bubbles in sparkling water will trap air in the dough, giving the pie a lighter texture, but still water will work fine as well. You can use 1 ounce pancetta or *guanciale* instead of sausage, or you can make this a vegetarian dish by eliminating the meat all together. If you adore cheese, add a quarter cup of ricotta or grated Cheddar cheese. The possibilities are endless. MAKES ONE 10 × 14-INCH PIE

# BRAISING GREENS PIE

### FOR THE FILLING

1 pound (453 g) mixed greens, such as chard, spinach, kale, and collard, thick ribs removed

4 ounces (113 g) loose sweet Italian sausage

1 small onion, minced

1 tablespoon extra-virgin olive oil

½ teaspoon fine sea salt

1 large egg

¾ cup (75 g) grated pecorino Romano cheese

### FOR THE DOUGH

3 cups (360 g) all-purpose einkorn flour

1 teaspoon fine sea salt

3 tablespoons (45 g) extra-virgin olive oil

½ cup (115 g) sparkling water

2 tablespoons dry white wine

Olive oil, for greasing

1 MAKE THE FILLING: Bring 2 quarts of water to a boil in a large pot. Add the greens and cook for 5 minutes until tender. Drain and let cool. Squeeze out the excess water and chop well.

2 In a medium skillet over medium heat, sauté the sausage and onion in the olive oil for 3 to 4 minutes until the sausage completely changes color, breaking up the large pieces. Add the greens and the salt and continue to cook for 2 minutes. Let cool, then beat in the egg and cheese.

3 MAKE THE DOUGH: In a medium bowl, combine the flour and salt. Add the olive oil and press together through your fingers until the dough is crumbly. Add the water and wine and knead the dough with your hands in the bowl until incorporated, then move to a clean work surface and knead for 1 minute until smooth. Place the dough back in the bowl and let rest for 10 minutes.

4 Preheat the oven to 375°F. Lightly grease a baking sheet with olive oil.

5 Divide the dough in half. Roll out one half, on a piece of parchment paper, to a 10 × 14-inch rectangle. Transfer the dough to the baking sheet. Spread the greens evenly over the dough, leaving a ½-inch border. Roll out the remaining dough to the same size and place it on top of the greens, stretching to fit with the bottom dough. Press down the edges with a fork to seal, then prick holes in the dough. Bake for 40 minutes until golden brown and crispy. Let cool before slicing.

MY CHILDREN ALWAYS TURNED up their noses at the vegetables in chicken pot pie, which surprised my pot-pie-loving self. I decided to change the recipe to include a different assortment of roasted vegetables, and to bake the chicken with rosemary before filling the pie to suit their tastes better. A simple homemade chicken broth adds rich flavor to the filling and the boiled chicken is also added to the pie. You can really taste the difference in flavor that the hearty einkorn flour makes in recipes like this one. SERVES 6 TO 8

# ROASTED ROOT VEGETABLE & CHICKEN COUNTRY-STYLE PIE

### FOR THE CHICKEN BROTH

2 chicken drumsticks

½ small onion

½ carrot

½ celery stalk

2 teaspoons fine sea salt

### FOR THE PIE CRUST

2½ cups (300 g) all-purpose einkorn flour

½ teaspoon fine sea salt

8 tablespoons (113 g) cold unsalted butter, cut into ¼-inch cubes

6 tablespoons ice water

### FOR THE PIE FILLING

2 tablespoons extra-virgin olive oil

8 ounces boneless, skinless chicken meat, cut into 1½-inch pieces

1 medium sweet potato, cut into ½-inch wedges

1 medium red onion, cut into ½-inch wedges

2 carrots, cut into ½-inch slices

1 parsnip or 3 purple potatoes, peeled and cut into ½-inch slices or wedges

3 sprigs of fresh rosemary

Salt and freshly ground black pepper

### FOR THE CREAM SAUCE

3 tablespoons unsalted butter

3 tablespoons all-purpose einkorn flour

½ cup (122 g) whole milk

Freshly ground black pepper, to taste

**1** MAKE THE CHICKEN BROTH: Bring 6 cups of water to a boil in a medium saucepan. Add the chicken, onion, carrot, celery, and salt. Bring to a boil, cover the pan, and simmer for 90 minutes. Strain the broth and strip the meat from the drumsticks for the filling.

**2** MAKE THE CRUST: In a large bowl, combine the flour and salt. Cut the butter into the flour mixture with a pastry blender. Add the ice water and squeeze the dough in your hands until it holds together. Knead for 1 minute on a clean work surface. Divide the dough in 2 pieces and flatten each into a disc. Wrap in plastic wrap and refrigerate for 30 minutes or overnight. (If refrigerating overnight, let come up to room temperature for 10 to 15 minutes to soften slightly before rolling.)

**3** Preheat the oven to 400°F.

**4** **MAKE THE FILLING:** Add the oil to a 9 × 13-inch baking pan. Add the chicken, then spread the sweet potato, onion, carrots, parsnip or potatoes, and rosemary on top. Season with salt and pepper. Bake for 30 minutes, stirring the vegetables and chicken after 15 minutes. Toss in the cooked chicken from the broth.

**5** **MAKE THE CREAM SAUCE:** Melt the butter in a medium saucepan over medium-low heat. Stir in the flour and cook for 30 seconds, whisking constantly. Slowly add 1 cup of the hot chicken broth, ½ cup at a time, whisking after each addition, until the mixture is smooth and begins to thicken. Add the milk and bring to a low simmer. Continue to whisk and cook on medium-low heat for 3 to 4 minutes until the mixture has thickened slightly. The cream will continue to thicken while baking. Remove from the heat and season with pepper.

**6** To assemble the pie, remove the dough from the refrigerator. On a floured piece of parchment paper, roll the first piece of the dough about 2 inches larger than the rim of your pie dish and about ⅛ inch thick, lifting and turning the dough with each roll. Place the dough in a 9-inch pie dish and gently press it into the bottom edges and up the sides. Add the chicken and vegetables. Pour the cream sauce on top. Roll out the top

crust in the same manner as the bottom. Place the top crust on top of the filling. Crimp or flute the edges together, and prick the crust with a fork.

**7** Bake for 35 to 40 minutes until the crust is golden brown and bubbly in spots. Allow the pie to cool for 30 minutes before serving.

**THIS IS A HEARTY** Tuscan-style soup that is typical of the Garfagnana region in the province of Lucca. There is a group of farmers in Garfagnana who are dedicated to preserving emmer, or *farro dicoccum,* as it is called in Latin. (In fact, you will often see emmer wheat berries labeled as farro.) Italians also refer to spelt and einkorn as farro, though einkorn does not have a deep crevice down the center of the grain and it is much smaller. For the best flavor, finish off this vegetarian soup with a drizzle of fresh extra-virgin olive oil and grated cheese and let rest for 30 minutes to an hour before serving. This is a large pot of soup that will taste even better reheated the next day.

SERVES 6 TO 8

# TUSCAN FARRO SOUP

1½ cups (300 g) einkorn wheat berries

¼ cup (50 g) extra-virgin olive oil

1 medium onion, minced

2 carrots, chopped

1 celery stalk, chopped

1 garlic clove, minced

1 cup (125 g) jarred crushed tomatoes

2½ teaspoons fine sea salt

2 medium red potatoes, diced small

½ bunch dinosaur kale, stems removed and chopped

One 4-inch sprig of fresh rosemary

3 fresh sage leaves

2 cups cooked cannellini beans

Freshly ground black pepper, to taste

1 cup (100 g) grated pecorino Romano cheese

**1** Add the wheat berries to a medium bowl. Cover with 3 cups of cold water and soak for 8 hours. Drain and rinse.

**2** In a large stockpot, add 2 tablespoons of the oil, the onion, carrots, celery, and garlic. Cook on medium-low heat for 3 minutes. Add the tomatoes and cook for 3 minutes more. Add 7 cups of water and the salt. Bring to a boil. Add the potatoes, kale, drained wheat berries, rosemary, and sage to the pot. Cover and simmer for 30 minutes. Add the beans and pepper and cook for 5 minutes more until the potatoes are soft. Turn off the heat and let cool for 15 minutes, covered.

**3** Stir in the remaining 2 tablespoons of olive oil and the grated cheese. Cover and let stand for 30 minutes before serving.

**EVERY NORTHERN ITALIAN** *nonna* surely makes *spezzatino,* slow-braised and tender chunks of beef cooked in wine and a bit of tomato sauce. My mother-in-law is the expert at preparing slow-cooked meat dishes like this one, so I consulted with her on this recipe. She uses a pressure cooker, which cuts back on time and cooks the meat to tender perfection. If you do not have a pressure cooker, no worries—I've scaled this recipe for a Dutch oven, where the meat should braise for a few hours on the stove. Though *spezzatino* is typically served over corn polenta, I have included a recipe for delicious whole grain einkorn polenta, which has a really nice flavor that balances the richness of meat. SERVES 4

# BEEF SPEZZATINO WITH EINKORN POLENTA

FOR THE BEEF STEW

2 tablespoons extra-virgin olive oil

2 pounds chuck roast, cut into 2-inch cubes

2 tablespoons unsalted butter

1 medium onion, minced

2 tablespoons all-purpose einkorn flour

2 carrots, diced small

1 celery stalk, diced small

¼ teaspoon herbes de Provence, or a pinch each of dried marjoram, rosemary, thyme, and oregano

2 bay leaves

2 teaspoons fine sea salt

¼ teaspoon freshly ground black pepper

½ cup dry white wine

½ cup jarred crushed or diced tomatoes

FOR THE POLENTA

1½ cups (300 g) einkorn wheat berries

1 teaspoon fine sea salt

**1** MAKE THE STEW: In a Dutch oven or heavy-bottomed pot, heat the oil on medium heat. When the oil is hot, add about 10 pieces of chuck roast to the pan without crowding. Cook the meat for about 10 minutes, turning it so that it browns on all sides. Set the first batch aside on a platter and continue browning the remaining pieces in small batches.

**2** Add the butter to the pot and heat, scraping up the browned meat drippings. Add the onion and cook for 2 minutes. Whisk in the flour. Add the browned chuck roast and stir so it is coated in the butter mixture. Add the carrots, celery, herbes de Provence, bay leaves, salt, and pepper. Add the wine and let evaporate for 1 minute. Mix in the tomatoes and ½ cup of water and cook uncovered until the mixture just begins to boil. Lower the heat to maintain a slow simmer. Cook on low heat with a lid slightly ajar for 1 to 3 hours, adding ½ cup of water after 30 minutes and more as needed.

**3 MAKE THE POLENTA:** Grind the wheat berries in a grain mill or in a high-powered blender to a medium coarse texture.

**4** Bring 3½ cups of water to a rolling boil in a medium saucepan. Add the salt and the ground wheat berries. Stir constantly with a wooden spoon until the mixture begins to boil. Lower the heat, cover, and cook on low for 15 minutes, stirring frequently. Uncover and cook for an additional 10 minutes, stirring constantly to avoid sticking.

**5** Add the polenta to a serving platter and spoon the *spezzatino* on top. Let stand for 5 minutes before serving.

ON SATURDAYS IN THE summertime, our family loves to go to the farmers' market for fresh fish, vegetables, and fruit. We eat lunch in the yard, and quite often these fish burgers are part of the ritual. This recipe is a great use of dry einkorn bread, and you can change up the fish to change the flavor: Try combining bluefish, striped bass, scallops, or shrimp. While I prefer to serve the patties on top of a salad, you could also serve them inside einkorn Hamburger Buns (see page 64). For parties, I like to form these into 1-inch-wide fish cakes and serve them with homemade tartar sauce. MAKES 6 BURGERS

# COD & SALMON BURGERS

1 cup (90 g) einkorn bread crumbs

¼ cup plain yogurt

¼ cup extra-virgin olive oil, plus more for greasing the pan

1 large egg

3 scallions (light green and white parts), chopped

2 tablespoons minced fresh dill

1 tablespoon minced fresh parsley

1 garlic clove, minced

1½ teaspoons fine sea salt

¾ pound (340 g) wild salmon fillet, skinned and cut into 1-inch pieces

½ pound (227 g) wild cod fish, cut into 1-inch pieces

6 thick slices provolone cheese

1 Add the bread crumbs, yogurt, 3 tablespoons of the oil, the egg, scallions, dill, parsley, garlic, and salt to a food processor and pulse until the ingredients are mixed well. Add the salmon and cod and process for 15 to 30 seconds until the fish is coarsely chopped and the mixture forms a ball.

2 Place a baking sheet in the oven and preheat to 400°F.

3 Pour the remaining 1 tablespoon oil into a small bowl. Divide the fish mixture into 6 equal portions. Dip your hands in the oil, then form 6 patties that are roughly 4 inches in diameter and ½ inch thick. (For perfectly round patties, press the fish mixture into a 3¾-inch round cookie cutter.) Place the patties on a sheet of parchment paper. If you are not planning on baking right away, you can wrap the uncooked patties in plastic wrap and inside a zip-top bag and store in the freezer for 1 month if the fish was not previously frozen. Thaw completely before cooking.

4 Remove the baking sheet from the oven and coat the pan with oil. Transfer the patties to the sheet and bake for 10 minutes, flipping halfway through the cooking time. Top with the slices of cheese and cook for 2 to 3 minutes more. Serve immediately.

NOTE: These burgers may also be grilled in a medium-hot grill for 3 minutes per side. They are delicate, so be careful when turning them on the grill.

# STREET
# FOOD

Sprouted Veggie Burgers, page 197

**WHEN I FIRST CAME TO ITALY, I WAS AMAZED AT THE FACT** that there was really just one type of cuisine. Italian food varies from town to town, region to region, but in essence, the ingredients and style of preparation are all very similar. Just as Italians hold on to their culinary traditions dearly, the same is true in other cultures. Growing up in the United States, I was exposed to many types of cultural cooking and I was blessed to meet friends from diverse ethnic backgrounds. Tasting these foods at their homes, especially Korean food during college, was an incredible experience. I have always been amazed at how tiny adjustments to the same ingredients, like adding a bit of fresh sage while cooking Tuscan beans, as opposed to adding cumin to Mexican, can create such diverse variations in flavor. I think it's important to keep your cooking as exciting as possible, so you should master at least a handful of recipes from other cultures.

This book ends with international street foods that are mouthwatering, fun, and worth celebrating. Maybe it is my secret hope that someday einkorn's comeback journey will make its way as far as street vendors in the great cities of the world. For now, to experience einkorn's versatility in international cuisines in the comfort of your own home, this chapter presents you with a diverse spectrum of flavors ranging from Refried Bean Chimichangas (page 198) to Einkorn Kibbeh with Minty Tzatziki (page 202) to Piadina (page 205). Einkorn delivered a newfound flavor and excitement to my kitchen while also giving my family the freedom to eat what we wanted without concern. Our journey with einkorn is now many years in the making, and we are looking forward to creating new food traditions with this ancient grain. The future of cooking with einkorn has just begun for all of us.

THIS RECIPE OFFERS EVERYTHING you are looking for in a veggie burger: the high amount of plant protein from the sprouted einkorn and beans without the saturated fat of ground beef. The patties may be formed, tightly wrapped, and frozen, then defrosted completely and baked at a later date. You can change up the vegetables and spices to your liking—some great flavor combinations might be shiitake mushrooms and leeks, asparagus and spring onions, or peppers and tomatoes; just be sure to add 2 cups of minced vegetables. Serve these on top of einkorn Hamburger Buns (see page 64; photograph on page 194). MAKES 8 VEGGIE BURGERS

# SPROUTED VEGGIE BURGERS

1½ cups (300 g) einkorn wheat berries

¾ cup (145 g) dried black beans

2 fresh sage leaves

2½ teaspoons sea salt

3 tablespoons extra-virgin olive oil, plus more for greasing the baking sheet

1 medium onion, minced

1 large carrot, minced

1 celery stalk, minced

1 medium zucchini, minced

1 garlic clove, minced

⅛ teaspoon ground turmeric

⅛ teaspoon dried oregano

⅛ teaspoon ground ginger

⅛ teaspoon dried thyme

1 egg, beaten (optional)

1 Sprout the wheat berries following the instructions on page 18, but do not dehydrate the grains. Add the beans to a medium bowl with 2 cups of water and soak for 8 hours.

2 Bring 4 cups of water to a boil. Add the soaked beans and sage and cook for 30 minutes. Add 1 teaspoon of the salt and cook for 10 minutes more until very tender. Drain the beans and discard the sage.

3 Steam the wheat berries in a medium saucepan fitted with a fan steamer, cooking for 10 minutes until soft. Set aside.

4 In a medium skillet, heat the oil on medium-low. Add the onion, carrot, celery, zucchini, garlic, turmeric, oregano, ginger, thyme, and 1 teaspoon of the salt. Cook for 3 minutes.

Add ¼ cup of water, cover, and cook for 8 minutes more until the vegetables have begun to soften. Set aside to cool for 5 minutes.

5 Grease a baking sheet. Preheat the oven to 375°F.

6 Combine the cooked vegetables, wheat berries, and beans with the remaining ½ teaspoon salt in a large bowl. Add half of the mixture to a food processor and process until the mixture is ground coarsely and sticks together. Add the processed mixture to a large bowl. Process the second batch and add to the bowl. Work the egg, if using, into the mixture with your hands until fully incorporated.

7 Divide the mixture into 8 packed ½-cup portions and form patties that are 3½ inches in diameter and nearly ¾ inch thick. Bake the burgers for 20 minutes, turning once after 15 minutes.

THE THOUGHT OF MEXICAN street food makes my mouth water. I have taken some liberties in creating these vegan chimichangas, based on a recipe I learned years ago from Annemarie Coblin's *The Natural Gourmet* cookbook. The added bonus is how crunchy and golden the leavened semi-whole grain einkorn dough is when fried. Serve as is, or with sour cream, salsa, and guacamole on the side. MAKES 12 CHIMICHANGAS

# REFRIED BEAN CHIMICHANGAS

2¼ cups dried pinto beans (see Note)

FOR THE DOUGH

¼ cup (60 g) Einkorn Sourdough Starter (page 13), or ⅛ teaspoon active dry yeast

¾ cup (177 g) warm water, at 100°F

3 tablespoons extra-virgin olive oil

2½ cups (300 g) all-purpose einkorn flour

1¼ cups (120 g) whole grain einkorn flour

1¼ teaspoons fine grain salt

FOR THE FILLING

1 bay leaf

1¼ teaspoons fine sea salt

3 tablespoons extra-virgin olive oil

1 medium onion, chopped

2 teaspoons ground cumin

1 teaspoon dried oregano

Pinch of cayenne pepper

Vegetable oil, for frying

**1** Soak the beans overnight or for 12 hours.

**2** MAKE THE DOUGH: Combine the starter or yeast with the water in a small bowl and mix until creamy. Mix in the olive oil.

**3** In a large bowl, combine the flours and salt. Add the wet mixture to the flour mixture and mix as much as you can with a spatula. Knead the dough with your hands in the bowl until it begins to hold together. Transfer to a clean work surface and knead until smooth and a bit sticky. Cover the bowl and proof for 3 to 5 hours at room temperature or in the refrigerator for 6 to 24 hours. (If the dough has been refrigerated, remove from

the refrigerator now so it will come to room temperature while you cook the beans.)

**4** MAKE THE FILLING: Drain the beans and place them in a medium saucepan. Add 5 cups of water and the bay leaf. Bring to a boil, then reduce the heat and cover the pot. Simmer for 50 minutes. Add 1 teaspoon of the salt and cook for 10 more minutes. Remove the pan from the heat, but do not drain the beans yet.

**5** In a large skillet, add the olive oil and onion. Sprinkle the cumin, oregano, cayenne, and the remaining ¼ teaspoon salt on top and cook on medium heat for 2 minutes. Transfer the cooked beans from the pot to the skillet with

a slotted spoon. Add ¾ cup of the bean cooking liquid and continue to cook for 5 minutes. Use a potato masher to purée the beans in the skillet while they cook. Add ½ cup of the bean cooking liquid and cook for 5 minutes until the water has evaporated and the beans are thick, stirring frequently. Set aside to cool for 30 minutes, stirring occasionally.

6 **SHAPE THE CHIMICHANGAS:** Divide the dough into 12 equal pieces. Roll out the first piece into a 7 × 8-inch rectangle. Fill the center with a wide strip of ½ cup of refried beans. Fold the short sides over the beans, then fold one long side to the center and roll the chimichanga to close. Place the chimichanga on parchment paper and repeat with the remaining dough and beans.

7 Line a wire rack with paper towels. Pour the vegetable oil into a frying pan to a depth of 1½ inches and heat the oil to 350°F. Cook 2 to 3 chimichangas in the oil for 2 minutes, turning as you cook, until each side is golden. Remove with a metal spatula or kitchen tongs and place on the cooling rack. Repeat with the remaining chimichangas, monitoring the temperature of the oil between batches. Allow to cool for 15 minutes before serving.

**NOTE:** Rather than make the beans from scratch, you can also use 5 cups canned beans, and 1¼ cups water or stock in place of the bean cooking liquid.

**ALTHOUGH THE TRADITION OF** salting cod comes from northern Europe, countries like Portugal, Spain, and Italy, where it is called *baccalà*, have embraced this ingredient. As a child, I loved my father's *baccalà*, which he stewed slowly in a tomato broth and served over polenta. I love this recipe, which is adapted from the fritters served at our annual town fair in Emilia-Romagna. The fish is soaked and then flaked into a simple batter made with flour and water. It will take 2 days to soak the salt out of the fish, so plan accordingly. The pieces do not always weigh exactly 1 pound, so I have given a range of weight that suits this amount of batter. MAKES ABOUT 30 FRITTERS

# SALT COD FRITTERS

1 to 1½ pounds (453 g to 680 g) salt cod

2 tablespoons extra-virgin olive oil

1 tablespoon dry white wine

2 tablespoons minced fresh parsley

2 tablespoons minced fresh chives

1¼ cups (295 g) warm water, at 100°F

½ cup (120 g) refreshed Einkorn Sourdough Starter (page 13), or ¼ teaspoon active dry yeast

2 cups (240 g) all-purpose einkorn flour

Vegetable oil, for frying

**1** Rinse the salt cod under warm water to remove the excess salt. Place the fish in a large bowl and add cold water to about 1 inch above the fillet. Cover and refrigerate for 2 days, changing the water twice a day.

**2** Place the fish in a large skillet with enough fresh water to cover the fillets. Bring to a simmer, then cover the skillet and cook on medium-low heat for 12 to 15 minutes until the fish flakes easily with a fork. Transfer the fish to a large bowl. Use a fork to break the fish apart in small chunks. Mix in the olive oil, wine, parsley, and chives.

**3** In a small bowl, mix the water with the starter or yeast until dissolved. Add the mixture to the fish. Sift the flour into the bowl and mix until the flour is thoroughly incorporated with the fish in a thick batter. Cover the bowl tightly with plastic wrap and let rest in the refrigerator for 3 to 4 hours.

**4** Line a dish with paper towels. Pour the vegetable oil into a frying pan to a depth of 1½ inches and heat the oil to 350°F. Drop heaping tablespoons of batter into the oil and cook for 1 minute, then turn the fritters over and continue cooking for 3 to 4 minutes, turning after each minute, until the fritters are lightly browned and crispy. Remove and let drain on the paper towels. Taste the first fritter and adjust the salt in the batter if necessary. Repeat with the remaining fritters, monitoring the temperature of the oil between batches.

**5** Allow the fritters to cool for 10 minutes before serving.

**EINKORN WHEAT BERRIES ARE** ideal for incorporating into meat-based dishes like meat loaf or these Lebanese kibbeh. I like to bake the kibbeh instead of frying them, simply because it is less labor intensive and is equally delicious. The kibbeh can be made ahead and baked right before serving, and it looks fantastic served on a bed of lettuce and topped with minty *tzatziki*, a light herb and yogurt dressing. MAKES 2 DOZEN KIBBEH

# EINKORN KIBBEH
# WITH MINTY TZATZIKI

### FOR THE KIBBEH

½ cup (100 g) einkorn wheat berries

1⅛ teaspoons sea salt

¼ cup (50 g) extra-virgin olive oil

1 cup finely chopped zucchini

10 fresh mint leaves, minced

1 medium onion, diced

8 ounces ground beef

8 ounces ground lamb

½ teaspoon ground cumin

⅛ teaspoon freshly ground black pepper

### FOR THE MINTY TZATZIKI

1 cup (235 g) plain yogurt

2 tablespoons extra-virgin olive oil

1 tablespoon fresh lemon juice

2 scallions (light green and white parts), finely chopped

1 garlic clove, minced

1 tablespoon minced fresh mint

1 tablespoon minced fresh parsley

¼ teaspoon fine sea salt

Lettuce leaves, for serving

**1** Soak the wheat berries in 1½ cups of water for 8 to 10 hours. Drain and rinse.

**2** MAKE THE KIBBEH: In a small saucepan, bring ⅔ cup (157 g) water to a rolling boil. Add ¼ teaspoon of the salt and the wheat berries and simmer, covered, on low heat for 35 minutes until tender. Remove from the heat and let stand, covered, for 5 minutes, then set aside to cool.

**3** In a medium frying pan over medium-low heat, sauté 2 tablespoons of the oil with the zucchini, mint, and ⅛ teaspoon of the salt for 5 minutes until tender. Set aside to cool.

**4** Place the cooked wheat berries in the bowl of a food processor, and process until soft and creamy; transfer the purée to a large bowl. (If the mixture does not become creamy in your food processor, then use a blender for the wheat berries.) Add the onion and 1 tablespoon of the oil to the food processor and pulse until chopped finely. Add the beef, lamb, cumin, pepper, and remaining ¾ teaspoon salt and process until the mixture becomes very fine. Transfer the meat mixture to the bowl and combine with the wheat berries. Return the mixture to the food processor and purée again until it is very smooth, pale in color, and has a super fine texture.

**5** Preheat your oven to 400°F with a baking sheet inside.

**6** Divide the meat mixture into 24 equal pieces. Roll the first piece in your hands to form a round meatball shape. With your index finger, push a small hole in the center of the ball and add 1 teaspoon of the zucchini mixture, pressing the zucchini into the meat. Cover the opening by folding over the meat to seal the filling inside, then smooth out the surface with your finger and shape it to look like an egg.

**7** Add the remaining 1 tablespoon of oil to the hot baking dish, then add the kibbeh. Bake for 20 minutes, turning once halfway through.

**8** MAKE THE TZATZIKI: Whisk together the ingredients in a medium bowl. Set aside in the refrigerator until ready to serve.

**9** To serve, spread the lettuce leaves on a platter, drizzle with the *tzatziki*, and place the kibbeh on top.

**MY HUSBAND AND I** both have grandparents who originated from towns along the Adriatic Sea—his from the town of Forlì, and mine from only an hour away, in Fano. On the Adriatic, beachgoers often stop for *piadina* made by street vendors, who are clearly noticeable in their signature pinstriped wooden huts. Essentially the tortilla of Italy, *piadina* are typically folded in half and stuffed with charcuterie or cheese but can also be used as bread to soak up hearty sauces. The round of dough may also be stuffed like a calzone with tomato sauce and cheese, folded, and sealed with a fork, then cooked in the same manner. MAKES 10 PIADINA

# PIADINA

¼ cup (60 g) refreshed Einkorn Sourdough Starter (page 13), or 1 teaspoon active dry yeast

1 cup (236 g) warm water, at 100°F

¼ cup (50 g) extra-virgin olive oil or leaf lard

4¼ cups (510 g) all-purpose einkorn flour, plus more for dusting

1½ teaspoons sea salt

**1** In a medium bowl, dissolve the starter or yeast in the water. Whisk in the oil or lard, then add the flour and sprinkle the salt on top. Mix the dough with a spatula until the flour mostly absorbs the water. Transfer the dough to a floured work surface and knead until smooth, about 2 minutes. Return the dough to the bowl and cover tightly with plastic wrap. Let the dough rest at room temperature for 2 hours if you are using yeast, 4 hours if you are using sourdough.

**2** Heat a cast-iron frying pan or griddle to medium-low heat for 10 minutes until thoroughly hot.

**3** Divide the dough into 10 pieces. Roll each piece into a tight ball and cover with plastic wrap. Dust the first piece with a little flour and use a rolling pin to roll into an 8-inch disc. Place each *piadina* on the ungreased pan (or 2 *piadina*, if you are using a large griddle). Cook the first side of each *piadina* for about 2 minutes until golden brown spots have formed on the bread, being careful not to let it burn. (Do not flip over until the first side is fully cooked.) Flip and continue to cook on the other side for 3 minutes. Line a basket with a clean kitchen towel and keep the *piadina* warm while you finish rolling out and cooking the remaining dough. Serve warm or at room temperature.

**4** Store in a plastic bag for up to 3 days or freeze for up to 1 month. Reheat in the toaster or oven.

**A CLASSIC SICILIAN-STYLE COMFORT** food, *arancini* are balls of rice that are breaded and fried with a spoonful of meat sauce, mozzarella, and peas in the center. I first saw locals eating *arancini* for breakfast with cappuccino in Sicily when traveling in college. At the time, I was hesitant to choose something savory over all of the amazing pastries that surrounded me, but they were definitely what the local crowd went for. Now I like to eat them as a main dish or appetizer. The first time you make this einkorn wheat berry version, you might have a hard time forming them, but they will hold together nicely during frying. MAKES 10 ARANCINI

# WHEAT BERRY ARANCINI

1 cup (200 g) einkorn wheat berries

1 teaspoon sea salt

1 tablespoon unsalted butter

½ cup (50 g) finely grated Parmigiano-Reggiano cheese

2 large eggs, beaten

2 tablespoons extra-virgin olive oil

½ small onion, minced

½ carrot, minced

1 garlic clove, minced

4 ounces sweet Italian sausage, removed from its casing, or ground meat

¼ cup jarred crushed or strained tomatoes

2 cups (180 g) bread crumbs (about four ½-inch-thick slices einkorn bread, cubed)

½ cup (60 g) all-purpose einkorn flour

Vegetable oil, for frying

**1** Place the wheat berries in a bowl covered in 3 cups of water and soak overnight. Drain and rinse the wheat berries.

**2** In a medium saucepan, bring 1¼ cups (295 g) of water to a boil. Add the wheat berries and ¼ teaspoon of the salt and simmer, covered, for 30 minutes. Remove from the heat and let the wheat berries rest in the covered pan for 15 minutes. Place the wheat berries in a large bowl. Stir in the butter and cheese and let cool for 15 minutes. Stir in 1 egg.

**3** In a medium skillet, heat the olive oil on medium-low heat. Add the onion, carrot, and garlic and cook for 4 minutes. Add

the sausage and cook until it changes color and begins to brown, about 4 minutes. Add the tomatoes and ½ teaspoon of the salt and simmer, covered, for 15 minutes.

**4** To make the bread crumbs, place the bread cubes in a food processor and pulse until very finely chopped. You will need 2 cups (180 g) bread crumbs for the *arancini*. Set up a breading station by arranging the flour, the remaining beaten egg mixed with the remaining ¼ teaspoon of salt, and the bread crumbs in 3 shallow bowls.

**5** To shape the *arancini*, spread 2 tablespoons of the wheat berries on the palm of one hand. Add 1 tablespoon of the meat sauce and

firmly press into the center. Spoon 2 more tablespoons of wheat berries on top to cover the sauce. Cup your hands and squeeze gently to form a loose ball.

**6** Holding the ball in one hand, dip your other hand in the flour. Toss and coat the outside of the ball, moving it from one hand to the other and continuing to dust and squeeze with your hands until you have a firm ball that is thoroughly coated. Proceed in the same manner with the egg, then finally

with the bread crumbs, until the *arancini* are completely and evenly coated. Place the breaded *arancini* on a baking sheet. Form the rest of the *arancini* in the same manner.

**7** Add 2 inches of vegetable oil to a deep frying pan. Heat the oil to 325°F and fry the *arancini* in batches for 3 minutes per side until they are deeply golden brown. Allow to cool for 15 minutes before serving.

I REMEMBER LOVING THE flavor of tabbouleh the first time I tasted it at a friend's home but was then totally surprised when I later made it on my own—I had never added so much fresh parsley to any recipe before. That's what fascinates me about Lebanese food: Its freshness and flavor is created with an abundance of fresh herbs, garlic, onions, and lemon juice and this creates a clean and healthy taste. Now, making this salad with sprouted einkorn wheat berries for my family creates a high-protein, antioxidant-packed dish that we all love to snack on. It's important to keep the tabbouleh from becoming soggy, which is why I soak the tomatoes in the salt brine to release their juices before mixing the salad. MAKES 6 CUPS

# SPROUTED EINKORN TABBOULEH

1 cup (200 g) einkorn wheat berries

2 pounds large tomatoes (about 4), diced small

4 teaspoons fine sea salt

4 bunches (12 ounces/340 g) flat-leaf Italian parsley

Small bunch of fresh mint leaves

1 medium red onion

Pinch of freshly ground black pepper

Pinch of allspice

Pinch of cinnamon

Pinch of cloves

Pinch of nutmeg

Pinch of coriander

Pinch of ground ginger

½ cup (122 g) lemon juice

¼ cup (50 g) extra-virgin olive oil

**1** Sprout the einkorn wheat berries following the instructions on page 18, but do not dehydrate the grains.

**2** Add the tomatoes to a medium bowl with 2 cups of water and 2 teaspoons of the salt and let soak for 30 minutes.

**3** Steam the wheat berries in a medium saucepan fitted with a fan steamer, cooking for 10 minutes until soft. Set aside to cool.

**4** Remove the stems from the parsley and mint. Wash and dry the herbs thoroughly in a salad spinner. Add the herbs to a food processor with the onion and process until

very finely minced. (If your food processor is not very powerful, mince the herbs with a knife.) Transfer the herbs to a large serving bowl. Drain the tomatoes, add to the salad spinner, and spin until very dry. Add to the bowl with the herbs. Add the wheat berries and mix until the ingredients are well combined.

**5** Season the wheat berry mixture with the remaining 2 teaspoons salt and the pepper, allspice, cinnamon, cloves, nutmeg, coriander, and ginger and mix well. Add the lemon juice and oil. Mix again and serve immediately. The tabbouleh may be refrigerated in an airtight container for up to 2 days. Serve chilled.

I WAS INTRODUCED TO Korean food during college at the home of my best friend. Sue's family had immigrated to the United States when she was small, and her mother was a fabulous cook. I had never tasted anything as good as *bulgogi*, homemade kimchi, and dumplings. This recipe makes an abundant amount of dumplings, but they go fast. When cooking the dumplings, be sure to cover the pan completely so they steam and cook evenly inside while the outside browns. MAKES ABOUT 60 DUMPLINGS

# KOREAN DUMPLINGS

FOR THE DUMPLINGS

½ pound green cabbage, shredded

2½ teaspoons fine sea salt

3⅓ cups (400 g) all-purpose einkorn flour, plus more for dusting

1 cup (236 g) boiling water

3 ounces ground pork

3 ounces ground beef

2 scallions (light green and white parts), finely chopped

1 garlic clove, minced

1 teaspoon minced peeled fresh ginger

2 teaspoons soy sauce

2 teaspoons toasted sesame oil

½ teaspoon ground white pepper

Vegetable oil, for frying and greasing

FOR THE DIPPING SAUCE

¼ cup (72 g) soy sauce

1 tablespoon rice vinegar

1 teaspoon toasted sesame oil

1 tablespoon sugar

**1** MAKE THE DUMPLINGS: Place the cabbage in a large bowl and cover with cold water. Add 2 teaspoons of the salt to the water and mix with your hands. Let stand for 20 minutes.

**2** Place the flour in a medium bowl and form a well in the center. Add the boiling water and mix together with a fork as much as you can. When the dough is cool enough to handle, knead it in the bowl until you have a shaggy and sticky dough. Cover the bowl with a plate and let rest at room temperature for at least 15 minutes.

**3** In a large bowl, combine the pork, beef, scallions, garlic, ginger, soy sauce, sesame oil, and pepper. Sprinkle the remaining ½ teaspoon salt on top. Pick up the cabbage by the handful, squeezing tightly to drain all of the soaking water and add to the meat mixture. Once all of the cabbage is added, squeeze all of the ingredients through your hands for about 2 minutes until the cabbage has wilted and the mixture has become compact. Set aside.

**4** Lightly flour a work surface. Transfer the dough to the work area and knead it until smooth. Divide the dough into 6 pieces, keeping them all covered in the bowl until rolling.

**5** To assemble the dumplings, lightly flour a work surface and transfer the first piece of dough to it. Dust the dough on both sides and roll to a 12-inch round that is no more than ¹⁄₁₆ inch thick. Use a 3-inch round biscuit cutter to cut out the dumpling wrappers. Lightly grease 2 baking sheets with vegetable oil.

**6** Place 1 teaspoon of filling in the center of one half of each wrapper, leaving the margin clean, and gently fold the wrapper in half. To seal the dumpling, lift the top half slightly to grasp, pinch the center together, then press the dough between the index finger and thumb on both hands. To crimp the dough, move it forward and press it to the bottom half to make 5 seams along the edge. If the dough becomes dry, brush the edge lightly with water before sealing. Continue forming all of the dumplings. Place them on the prepared baking sheets. At this point, if you want to freeze the dumplings, place the baking sheets in the freezer. Once the dumplings are frozen solid, transfer them with a metal spatula to a sealable plastic bag and freeze for up to 3 months.

**7** MAKE THE DIPPING SAUCE: In a small bowl, combine the soy sauce, rice vinegar, sesame oil, and sugar with 1 tablespoon water and mix until the sugar dissolves. Place the sauce alongside a large serving platter.

**8** To cook the dumplings, heat ½ teaspoon of vegetable oil in a large nonstick frying pan on medium-low heat. Add a quarter of the dumplings to the hot oil, making sure they all touch the bottom of the pan without

overcrowding. Turn the heat down to low and cover the pan. Cook for 3 minutes per side (let frozen dumplings come to room temperature before cooking) until the dumplings are nicely browned all over. Lift the dumplings out of the skillet with kitchen tongs and place on a serving platter. Continue pan-frying the rest of the dumplings, wiping the skillet and adding ½ teaspoon of vegetable oil with each batch, then cooking in the same manner. Serve right away with the dipping sauce.

**MY HUSBAND AND I** started our work in food by running a small deli in Connecticut for a year in 1990. While brainstorming the menu, we made a list of authentic Italian foods that we could prepare and serve, like homemade tortelloni and *piadina*, as well as cappuccino (still a novelty back then). While my brother and a friend agreed all of these Italian specialties were nice, they insisted that sub sandwiches be included on the menu. So, along with selling Italian specialties, we ended up doing business also as a grinder shop, as they are referred to in New England. Occasionally, I fall back on that time and prepare a giant sandwich for friends, now with einkorn bread. If your oven is not large enough for a 24-inch loaf, you can shape it to the length that will fit and make it wider, or bake 2 loaves and divide the fillings between them. SERVES 10 TO 12; MAKES ONE 24-INCH SANDWICH ROLL

# PARTY-SIZE
## SUBMARINE SANDWICH

### FOR THE BREAD

1 batch Sourdough Levain (page 14) or Yeast Levain (page 14)

1½ cups (354 g) warm water, at 100°F

2 tablespoons extra-virgin olive oil

2 tablespoons sugar

6½ cups (780 g) all-purpose einkorn flour, plus more for dusting

2 teaspoons fine sea salt

### FOR THE FIXINGS

½ cup extra-virgin olive oil

¼ cup red wine vinegar

1 tablespoon dried oregano

12 ounces thinly sliced provolone cheese

10 ounces thinly sliced roasted turkey

10 ounces thinly sliced ham

8 to 10 ounces thinly sliced Genoa salami

6 ounces thinly sliced prosciutto

4 large tomatoes, thickly sliced

1 small head iceberg lettuce, thinly shredded

½ small head cabbage, thinly shredded

Salt and freshly ground black pepper

**1** MAKE THE BREAD: In a medium bowl, mix together the levain, water, oil, and sugar until creamy. In a large bowl, combine the flour and salt. Add the wet mixture to the dry mixture and mix with a spatula as much as you can. Knead the mixture in the bowl with your hands until it forms a rough ball. Lightly flour a work surface. Transfer the dough to the work area and knead for 2 minutes until it is smooth and a bit sticky. Place back in the bowl, cover with a plate, and let rest for 15 minutes.

**2** Turn the dough (see page 15) 3 times at 15-minute intervals. Cover the bowl tightly with plastic wrap and let proof at room temperature

for 3 to 5 hours or in the refrigerator for up to 12 hours.

**3** Transfer the dough to a lightly dusted work surface. Dust lightly with flour and knead the dough a few times to smooth it out. Tuck and fold the dough into a large log that measures 12 inches. Cover the log with plastic wrap and let rest for 15 minutes.

**4** Roll the log into a long loaf that measures 24 inches, or as long as you can fit in your oven. Press down on the loaf to flatten so it is no more than 3 inches in height. Line a baking sheet with parchment paper and place the loaf in the center. Oil a piece of plastic wrap and cover the loaf. Let proof for 90 minutes.

**5** Fill a baking dish with 1½ inches of water and place in the oven. Preheat the oven to 425°F.

**6** Slash the loaf in ¼-inch-deep diagonals to the width of the bread. Bake for 45 minutes until golden brown. Transfer the loaf to a rack to cool for 2 hours.

**7** MAKE THE FIXINGS AND ASSEMBLE: Slice the bread in half lengthwise. Combine the oil, vinegar, and oregano in a small bowl. Brush both sides of the bread with half of this dressing. Layer the cheese, turkey, ham, salami, and prosciutto on the bread, add the tomatoes, then cover with the shredded lettuce and cabbage. Pour the remaining oil and vinegar mixture over the lettuce and cabbage, and season with salt and abundant pepper. Close the top and serve within 1 to 2 hours.

**CRÊPES ARE THE STREET** food of Paris as well as of other French cities. Vendors make savory crêpes filled with ham and cheese or sweet crêpes filled with jam or chocolate and dusted with powdered sugar. You may make the batter up to a day before cooking and store it in the refrigerator. The crêpes will hold up very well when stacked on a plate, so do not be concerned about keeping them separated while you cook them. However, if you want to refrigerate them for the next day, place a piece of parchment paper in between each crêpe. MAKES 8 CRÊPES

# CRÊPES

2 large eggs

1 cup (244 g) whole milk

1 cup (120 g) all-purpose einkorn flour

2 tablespoons unsalted butter, melted, plus more for greasing the pan

1 tablespoon sugar

¼ teaspoon fine sea salt

**1** To make the crêpes, add the eggs, milk, flour, butter, sugar, and salt to a blender or food processor. Process for 45 seconds until the mixture is smooth and foamy. Pour the batter through a fine mesh strainer to a medium bowl or pitcher. Cover and refrigerate for at least 30 minutes.

**2** Lightly coat a 10-inch nonstick skillet or crêpe pan with butter and set over medium heat until the pan is hot. Add a scant ¼ cup of the batter and use a crêpe spreader, or tilt the pan in a circular motion, to completely cover the bottom of the skillet until you have a roughly 8-inch round. Cook for 30 to 45 seconds until the underside of the crêpe is golden brown, then lift the crêpe with a rubber spatula, grasp with your fingers, and flip. Cook the other side for 1 minute more. Place the crêpe on a plate and continue with the rest of the batter.

TRADITIONALLY, SOFT GERMAN PRETZELS are dipped in a lye solution right before baking. Thanks to an article in the *New York Times*, I started using baking soda instead. I learned that heating the baking soda in the oven for about 1 hour raises its pH, which promotes the Maillard reaction that gives pretzels a characteristically deep brown color, unique texture, and authentic flavor. This recipe can be used to make pretzel buns by dividing the dough into 8 pieces and rolling them into round rolls instead of shaping into a pretzel. MAKES 10 PRETZELS

# SOFT GERMAN PRETZELS

1 batch Sourdough Levain (page 14) or Yeast Levain (page 14)

½ cup plus 2 tablespoons (148 g) warm water, at 100°F

1 teaspoon pure maple syrup

4 cups (480 g) all-purpose einkorn flour

1¼ teaspoons fine sea salt

3 tablespoons unsalted butter, melted and cooled

⅔ cup (100 g) baking soda

Coarse sea salt or rock salt, for dusting

**1** In a medium bowl, combine the levain, water, and maple syrup. In a large bowl, combine the flour and salt. Add the wet mixture to the flour and mix with a spatula as much as you can. Add the butter and knead in the bowl with your hands until the dough holds together in a firm ball. Cover with a plate and let rest at room temperature for 15 minutes. Turn the dough (see page 15) once and then tightly seal the bowl with plastic wrap. Let rest for 3 hours.

**2** Brush a long piece of parchment paper lightly with oil. Divide the dough in 10 pieces, then roll each piece into a tight ball. Use your hands to roll each ball into a 22-inch strip of dough that is much thicker in the center and has tapered ends. Form each strip into a long U shape. Lift up both ends and cross one over the other 2 times, then bring the ends to the bottom of the oval and press on each side, leaving the

tip up slightly. Place the shaped pretzel on the prepared parchment and repeat with the remaining dough. Cover with oil-brushed plastic wrap and let rest at room temperature for 30 to 60 minutes. It is important to catch them just before the surface of the dough has visible bubbles.

**3** Preheat the oven to 275°F. Spread the baking soda in a 9 × 13-inch glass or ceramic baking dish. Bake the baking soda for 1 hour.

**4** Remove the dish from the oven, then increase the heat to 475°F. Line 2 clean baking sheets with parchment paper.

**5** Add 4 cups of cold water to a medium bowl and whisk in the baking soda. Add 6 cups of cold water to a second medium bowl for the rinse. Working in batches of 2 or 3 pretzels, immerse the pretzels in the baking soda solution for 2 minutes, keeping them submerged, and

turning after one minute. Lift each pretzel out with a spoon and dip quickly into the clean water to remove excess baking soda. Arrange the pretzels on the prepared baking sheet so that they are not touching, and sprinkle lightly with coarse salt.

**6** Bake for 14 to 16 minutes until the pretzels are deep brown. Let cool in the pan for 10 minutes before serving.

**THE DOUGH FOR THESE** Latin fried doughnuts is prepared in the same manner as cream puffs, and that type of preparation suits einkorn very well. Light and irresistibly crunchy, with a dusting of cinnamon sugar, these pastries are a crowd-pleaser. You must have a wide-open star tip for your pastry bag to prepare these properly—smaller tips will cause the dough to crack when it expands during cooking, and larger tips will make the strip of dough too thick and the center will not cook properly. MAKES 3 DOZEN CHURROS

# CHURROS

FOR THE CHURROS

2 cups (240 g) all-purpose einkorn flour

2 tablespoons sugar

½ teaspoon fine sea salt

1 cup (244 g) whole milk

4 tablespoons (56 g) unsalted butter

3 large eggs

Vegetable oil, for frying

FOR DUSTING

½ cup (100 g) sugar

1 teaspoon ground cinnamon

⅛ teaspoon fine sea salt

**1** MAKE THE CHURROS: In a small bowl, mix together the flour, sugar, and salt.

**2** In a medium saucepan, bring the milk and butter with 1 cup (236 g) water almost to a boil on medium heat. Add the flour mixture all at once. Continue to cook on medium, maintaining the mixture at a temperature just below boiling, stirring vigorously with a wooden spoon. The mixture will leave the sides of the pan and form a stiff ball after about 1 minute. Continue to press on the dough and cook for 1 minute more, being careful not to let the mixture get hot enough to bubble or brown.

**3** Transfer the dough to the bowl of a standing mixer and let cool for 10 minutes. Add 1 egg and mix on medium until the mixture goes

from clumpy to smooth, about 30 seconds. Continue with each egg in the same manner. Scoop the dough into a pastry bag fitted with a #827 open star tip.

**4** Heat 2 inches of oil for frying in a deep skillet to 375°F. Pipe 5-inch-long strips of dough into the hot oil, using a knife to cut off the end. Fry for 3 to 4 minutes, until deep golden and crispy, turning each strip after 2 minutes so that they brown evenly; drain on paper towels.

**5** FOR DUSTING: Combine the sugar, cinnamon, and salt in a baking dish. Roll the cooked churros in the sugar mixture to coat. These are best if eaten within 3 hours of frying. The dough may be prepared in advance and refrigerated for up to 5 hours, then brought to room temperature before frying.

STREET FOODS HAVE BEEN a part of Latin American culture for hundreds of years. Of Spanish origin, empanadas are savory pastry pockets that are filled with ground meat that is simmered with tomatoes, peppers, onion, and spices. You can also add sliced green olives to the filling, peppers, and boiled eggs. What I like about the empanada dough is that it varies from the normal *pâte brisée* way of combining cold butter and water with flour and refrigerating the dough. Here the dough is mixed with warm water, left out at room temperature, and rolled out while still warm. When you roll out the dough, remember not to roll too thin or the pocket will not be strong enough to hold the filling. This dough may also be stuffed in many ways for delicious baked hand-held pockets, like spinach and feta, chicken and broccoli, or pepperoni and tomato sauce. MAKES 12 EMPANADAS

# EMPANADAS

FOR THE FILLING

3 tablespoons extra-virgin olive oil

1 medium onion, minced

2 jalapeño peppers, seeded and thinly sliced

1 garlic clove, minced

1 teaspoon ground cumin

1 teaspoon ground oregano

¼ teaspoon cayenne pepper

8 ounces lean ground beef

½ cup (130 g) jarred crushed or diced tomatoes

¾ teaspoon fine sea salt

½ cup pitted and sliced green olives (optional)

2 hard-boiled eggs, peeled and sliced (optional)

FOR THE DOUGH

2 cups (240 g) all-purpose einkorn flour, plus more for dusting

1 teaspoon fine sea salt

½ teaspoon baking powder

3 tablespoons leaf lard or cold unsalted butter, cut into ¼-inch cubes

1 large egg, beaten

⅓ cup (79 g) warm water, at 100°F

1 large egg white, for the egg wash

**1** MAKE THE FILLING: Heat the oil in a large skillet on medium-low heat. Add the onion, jalapeños, garlic, cumin, oregano, and cayenne and cook for 2 minutes. Add the beef and cook for 4 to 5 minutes, breaking it up with a spatula, until the meat has lost its raw color. Add the tomatoes and salt. Cover the skillet, turn the heat down to low,

and cook for 12 minutes. Turn off the heat and mix in the olives and eggs, if using. Set aside to cool.

**2** MAKE THE DOUGH: Combine the flour, salt, and baking powder in a large bowl. Using a pastry blender, cut the lard or butter into the flour mixture until it resembles coarse sand. Add the

beaten egg and use a fork to blend it into the flour mixture. Add the water and knead the dough with your hands in the bowl until the mixture forms a ball. Transfer the dough to a clean work surface and knead for 1 minute until smooth. Return the dough to the bowl, cover with plastic wrap, and let rest for 15 minutes at room temperature.

**3** Preheat the oven to 350°F. Line a baking sheet with parchment paper.

**4** Divide the dough into quarters and place back in the covered bowl. Lightly flour a work surface and transfer the first piece of dough to it. Roll out the dough to a 10-inch round that is about $\frac{1}{16}$ inch thick. Using a 5-inch-round pastry cutter or a wide-mouthed glass, cut out two 5-inch rounds. Place the dough scraps back in the bowl.

Repeat with the remaining dough scraps to make more rounds, rerolling the dough as necessary.

**5** Lift 1 round of dough and flour the work surface lightly if needed. Place 2 tablespoons of filling in the middle of one half of the round. Fold the dough to create a half-moon shape. To seal the empanadas with a rope pattern, starting at one end, lift the edge of the dough and use your thumb to fold and pinch the dough over itself every $\frac{1}{8}$ inch. Place the shaped empanada on the baking sheet and proceed with forming the remaining empanadas.

**6** Bake for 15 minutes. In a small bowl, beat the egg white with 1 tablespoon water. Brush the egg wash on each empanada, and bake for 15 minutes more. Let cool for 15 minutes before serving.

# ACKNOWLEDGMENTS

Thank you, Mom and Dad. I still cry when I think about how short our time was together, but I know you are with me every day.

To my husband, Rodolfo, everything that I have accomplished in my adult life was done with your help. Thank you.

To my daughters, Giulia and Livia, all of this is for you. As little girls, you watched with tears when I burned my arm as I made your first lemon meringue pie. Little did you know that much of Mom's time would be spent working in the kitchen, after working all day. You have had patience and played a huge role in making decisions about each recipe in this book. We have a special life together. May your future be bright and beautiful.

To my brother, Mike, you have always believed in me and without your support, jovial, bionaturæ, einkorn, and this book would not have been possible.

I would like to thank my mother-in-law, *la nonna*, for teaching me so much. You are an epic woman.

To the amazing staff at my company, thank you for making dreams a reality every day. I won't mention names, because you are each equally important to me.

Thank you to Jessica Nocentini for your support and tenacity throughout the final photo shoot.

*Grazie* to Paolo Ghidi of Agriturismo San Polo and Gianni Berna of La Maridiana Alpaca for allowing me to take many of the photos in this book at your beautiful farms.

I would like to thank everyone directly involved in helping me to complete this book—especially Clarkson Potter, for supporting einkorn wheat as a new and important ingredient for the gluten sensitive: my editors, Jessica Freeman-Slade and Ashley Phillips, you both have been a joy to work with and have made the process of creating my first cookbook a very positive experience; Joyce Wong, production editor; Philip Leung, production manager; LaTricia Watford, designer; Doris Cooper, editorial director; and Aaron Wehner, publisher. A sincere thanks to my agent, Danielle Svetcov; my recipe tester, Tara Duggan; and photographer Clay McLachlan for your key roles in making this book a beautiful reality.

Lastly, the greatest thank-you goes to the consumers and retail stores who have supported our company's products for many years, especially einkorn. You have made my work possible and I am forever grateful.

# INDEX

NOTE: Page references in *italics* indicate photographs.